Created Images

Created Images

Attitudes That Show

MARCEAL CLARK

Created Images

by Marceal Clark

Hazelwood, MO 63042-2299

Cover design by Lance Reed

All Scripture quotations in this book are from the King James Version of the Bible unless otherwise identified.

Printed in United States of America

Printed by

WAP

Library of Congress Cataloging-in-Publication Data

Clark, Marceal.
Created images : attitudes that show / Marceal Clark.
p. cm.
ISBN 1-56722-137-8
1. Beatitudes—Devotional literature. 2. Christian life. 3. Attitude (Psychology)—Religious aspects—Christianity.
BT382.C56 1995
241.5'3—dc20 95-31170
CIP

To Keith,

Mender of shattered dreams,

Healer of wounded emotions.

When God created you

He made a gift just for me.

Contents

Foreword

What impression do we give?

We often say that our impression of a certain person is good or bad. How do we receive such an impression? It is not just from his words, nor even from his actions. A mysterious something expresses itself while he is speaking or acting. It is this that gives us the impression.

We may be able to control our speech or action, but we are unable to restrain that which expresses our nature. What we are, we cannot but reveal.

1

Created Images: Stripping the Facade

This is the age of created images. An image is a false wall screening from view the inner person. We save face with created images. Others need not know that we don't have it all together, we reason.

A created image is a mask that covers, conceals, and disguises our innermost selves. The vulnerable inner person retreats when masks are donned. Loneliness is covered by loudness. A tender and disillusioned heart is concealed most effectively behind a "don't care" attitude.

Larry is a loud, brash individual. His loudness is a created image masking his true self. The public views him as a coarse person when, in reality, behind the mask of loudness lies his true inner self of loneliness. Larry tries to cover that loneliness with his created image of macho loudness.

John has been hurt in a relationship of life. While he licks his wounds, he covers them with a "don't care" attitude. The "don't care" mask disguises a tender and wounded heart that recoils with the fear of being hurt again.

In the working world, we confront all sorts of faces hiding behind masks. Barney, the office "wolf" that every girl tries to avoid, is really covering up a deep sense of insecurity. Martha, the girl who flirts with all the guys, doesn't want the world to know of her deep-seated fear of going through life unloved. Rosey, the office gossip, is really telling you that she has a low self-esteem and must resort to gossip in order to feel important. Those who stab others in the back under the guise of friendship usually harbor a guilty conscience.

The pastor may sometimes present the created image of "all's well" when deep inside anxiety and anguish over his flock may dwell. The insensitive will pick up on the mask and do nothing, but the sensitive will go to God in prayer asking for guidance, peace, and calmness for him.

Nonverbal Languages

Scientists have discovered that more than half of all communication is nonverbal. They go so far as to say that the importance of the nonverbal component of a conversation far outweighs the impact of the actual words spoken.

When the verbal and nonverbal messages from a person do not correspond, most people respond to and believe the nonverbal signals rather than the spoken message, no matter how persuasively it is said. By listening to the nonverbal aspects of speech—volume, pitch, rate, and vocal quality—we determine a person's true state of mind.

A nervous person often speaks in a high-pitched quaver. However, a person in the throes of deep emotion will often speak in a low-pitched, husky voice.

The volume at which one speaks also relays a message. For example, a whisper indicates intimacy, closeness. A person speaking unnecessarily loudly is implying, "Hey, look at me."

The rate at which one speaks conveys meaning as well. Someone who babbles on at ninety miles a minute is excited about something important in his life even though his words may be only describing the Big Mac he had for lunch that day. A person speaking in an exaggerated slow rate may be implying that you're not getting what he's saying.

If someone would say to you, "I love you," with an indifferent tone in his voice, more than likely you would discard the words spoken and pick up on the indifferent quality of his voice.

There are other nonverbal "languages" that we learn how to "speak." If we are sensitive to the created images of others we learn how to pick up on "face language." We respond to face language every day without being aware of it.

Have you ever been cut down dead by the glance of another? Have you been stared down by a strong-willed individual? Have you ever heard the complaint, "He looks down his nose at me"? Have you heard the expression, "She speaks volumes with her eyes"? These are all responses to the subtle messages conveyed by facial features.

A person may find it easy to lie with words, but what's in his heart eventually shows. The body, face, and tone of voice speak an instinctive "language" that he cannot silence.

Ministering to the Real Person

To be able to minister to the wounded spirit of a person rather than to the mask that covers is truly a Christlike attribute. Jesus Himself looked beyond the facade and ministered to the real. To follow the Master is to minister to the inner person.

By using tact with Barney, the office "wolf," we can strip away the facade and minister to his sense of insecurity. We must show him how God and Christians can handle his insecurities because the church is built on a solid foundation—the Rock, Christ Jesus.

When dealing with the flirt, the office gossip, and the back stabber, our ability to bolster self-esteem will make a difference in how these persons view themselves and, consequently, how they view God and others.

Anger, hatred, and resentment are usually only masks that disguise broken relationships. Instead of concentrating on the venom unleashed by these emotions, we can find ways to minister to the real problem, the broken relationship: why it happened, what could have prevented it from happening, how to put it back together again.

Remember Larry, the loud, coarse person? If we care about him, we can learn how to probe beneath his obnoxious mask and minister to his loneliness. Larry himself may not be aware of the real culprit lurking behind his created image of loudness or brashness. But with a little prayer and insight, we can help him understand his underlying emotions and true feelings, thereby helping him to combat his loneliness.

John's "don't care" attitude can be stripped away when we show him that true love hurts. He needs to know that building a wall around his heart will shield himself from further hurt but will also shield himself from love. By introducing him to the perfect love of the Savior, we can lead him to a genuine haven of safety. Our tact in dealing with John may cause his protective "don't care" shield to melt away and he may once again reach out for a loving relationship in his life.

Facing Our Own Masks

When the face we present to others does not correspond with what is going on in our heart, we need to examine the mask and examine our inner feelings. If bitterness lurks inside but we attempt to hide it behind a nonchalant, "you-won't-get-a-chance-to-hurt-me-again" attitude we must find ways to strip away the mask, puncture the diseased attitude, and let all the poison-infested feelings drain away.

Infection must heal from the inside out. Simply applying balm to the outside is not enough. When we attempt to soothe our feelings by applying the balm of "I'll get even," the bitterness is still there lurking deep within. Only when we strip away the soothing mask of "someone must pay," probe deep inside, and then let the scalpel of mercy and forgiveness lance the boil of bitterness will healing come. As the poison drains out of our system through mercy and forgiveness, fractured relationships are restored and once again what is in our heart will manifest itself in our life. Mercy and forgiveness in the heart will not put on a mask of "I'll get even with you." Mercy and forgiveness present only one face to the beholder: one that is transparent.

Learn to Interpret Messages

If we will take the time to interpret and understand the messages transmitted by others, not only by their words but by their facial expressions, movements, and vocal quality, we will be able to uncover their true thoughts and underlying emotions, thereby ministering to their real needs rather than to the masks they wear and the created images they have made for themselves. In so doing, we are following the Master.

The World's False Wall

Just as Barney, Larry, and John have built a false wall around their true selves, the world has constructed a false wall around the teachings of Jesus. In the fifth chapter of Matthew Jesus has given us what we call the Beatitudes. But instead of these "beautiful attitudes" of Jesus that should be the core of our inner self, the world has instituted its counterfeit for the genuine. The world has built a created image, a false wall, screening from view the inner person Jesus intended us to be. As with Barney, Larry, John, and the others, it is our responsibility to strip away this facade and unmask the genuine, letting the attitudes that show in our lives be those Jesus intended instead of the created images instituted by humanity.

Beatitudes of Jesus (Matthew 5:3-12)

1. "Blessed are the poor in spirit . . ."
2. "Blessed are they that mourn . . . "

3. "Blessed are the meek . . . "
4. "Blessed are they which do hunger and thirst after righteousness . . . "
5. "Blessed are the merciful . . . "
6. "Blessed are the pure in heart . . . "
7. "Blessed are the peacemakers . . . "
8. "Blessed are they which are persecuted for righteousness' sake . . . "
9. "Blessed are ye, when men shall revile you . . . for my sake . . . "

World's False Attitudes

1. "Blessed are those know-it-alls who have all the answers: for they will be smug and satisfied."
2. "Blessed are those who run from pain, seeking to make life simply fun and games."
3. "Blessed are the egotistical, vain, and self-centered: for they shall view the world from their lofty perch."
4. "Blessed are those who ignore God's laws: for they shall receive the applause of the world."
5. "Blessed are those who judge: for they shall get even."
6. "Blessed are the gossipers: for they shall be rewarded by seeing reputations destroyed."
7. "Blessed are the agitators: for they will transfer their discontentment to others."
8. "Blessed are those who conform to the crowd: for they will blend in."
9. "Blessed are those who have shallow faith: for when they are accused of being a Christian there will not be enough evidence to convict them."

Blessed: Happy

In the Beatitudes of Jesus (Matthew 5:3-12) the word "blessed" appears many times. The Greek word for "blessed" means "happy."

1. "Blessed [happy] are the poor in spirit."
2. "Blessed [happy] are they that mourn."
3. "Blessed [happy] are the meek."

Why are they happy? The last part of the verses perhaps is the key: they shall inherit the earth, shall be comforted, shall be filled. "Shall" is a promise. We have the promise that if we conform to the first part of the verses, obstacles *shall* disappear. The promises of happiness in these verses do not relate only to the hereafter, when we know for certain that all pain and sorrows will be dissolved, but relate to our everyday lives if we will reach out, claim them, and see them fulfilled.

If we strip away the facade of the world's created images, unmask the inner core of Jesus' teachings, and exhibit the attitudes He intended, true happiness will come.

The founding fathers of our nation spoke of "life, liberty, and the pursuit of happiness." The pursuit: does this mean that happiness is never apprehended? Never obtained, but continually pursued?

What actually is happiness? Is it contentment or merely an absence of strife? A zest for living or just an absence of problems? Happiness cannot be summoned. It cannot be demanded. Rather, it is an inward singing that cannot be silenced by outward negative circumstances. It is the byproduct of a growing relationship between us and God.

Attitudes That Show

In the following chapters we will study the attitudes

that show in our lives. Do we exhibit the created images the world has constructed? If so, we must find ways to strip them away, unmask the inner person Jesus intended us to be, and then exemplify these "beautiful attitudes" for others to see.

In so doing, blessed (happy) are we!

2

Humility or Pride

The world's version:
"Blessed are those know-it-alls who have all the answers: for they will be smug and satisified."

Jesus' version:
"Blessed are the poor in spirit: for theirs is the kingdom of heaven."

You know them as well as I. They are the ones who know everything about everything. Broach any subject and they are the expert. They know how to build a fence, bake a cake, overhaul a car, program computers, be a doctor, dentist, pharmacist, politician, pastor, and mother. They are the know-it-alls of this world.

"Don't do it that way, do it this way," she said. I was programming my memory typewriter, a job I had been doing successfully for many years. With a flick of her wrist, she erased all the memory that I had painstakingly entered.

"Er . . . sorry," she murmured. "I made a mistake."

Know-it-alls do not usually apologize, but this one did. Maybe it was because she saw the look on my face.

Know-it-alls can always do a better job than the expert:

1. "My doctor should have prescribed so and so."
2. "The mechanic put the wrong part in my car. It should have been such and such."
3. "The cake you made would have tasted better if you had done thus and so."
4. "In order to balance the federal budget, the president should do this and that."
5. "The pastor would be more effective if he did more of this and less of that."
6. "You're planting those tomatoes wrong. This is the way you do it!"

Mr. Know-it-all was at the dentist's office being fitted for a bridge. He was complaining. "Your fees are too high. I could do the job myself. All you're going to do is take a little of this and a little of that, mix it together, and plop it in my mouth. Why should I pay such exorbitant prices for a tiny bit of gold and wire?"

The dentist excused himself for a few minutes and when he returned he had a small brown paper sack in his hand. He handed the paper sack to Mr. Know-it-all and said, "I'm sorry. I didn't understand the situation. I didn't realize that you wanted the do-it-yourself special."

Know-it-alls have all the answers to all problems. If you don't believe it, just ask them. According to them, if you do things their way, all life's complex problems will be solved.

But Jesus said, "Blessed are the poor in spirit," the humble. Jesus knew it is against our human nature to be humble. Humility is the opposite of pride—the opposite of a boastful, know-it-all attitude. Humility means possessing a modest nature; not calling attention to oneself; being inconspicuous; not gaudy; unpretentious; not bold or forward.

Humility is the lesson of the familiar parable of the Pharisee and the publican:

"Two men went up into the temple to pray; the one a Pharisee, and the other a publican. The Pharisee stood and prayed thus with himself, God, I thank thee, that I am not as other men are, extortioners, unjust, adulterers, or even as this publican. I fast twice in the week, I give tithes of all that I possess. And the publican, standing afar off, would not lift up so much as his eyes unto heaven, but smote upon his breast, saying, God be merciful to me a sinner. I tell you, this man went down to his house justified rather than the other: for every one that exalteth himself shall be abased; and he that humbleth himself shall be exalted" (Luke 18:10-14).

The Pharisee's pride in his own goodness blocked God's blessings. He was so busy patting himself on the back for not being like other people that it never occurred to him he was not much like God either. In contrast, the contrite publican (tax collector) recognized the vast gulf between God and himself, and consequently the Bible says he "went down to his house justified."

It is not human nature to be humble. We want to stand up and shout our accomplishments, our goodness, our righteousness, our knowledge. Yet it is plain that Jesus wants those who love Him to defy their own pride and boastfulness. Moreover, our self-righteousness stands in the way of our prayers. Like the Pharisee, we are so busy telling God how good we are (we don't do this and we don't do that) that we fail to see how we are blocking His blessings. Assuredly, humility is a prerequisite to answered prayer.

A preacher once said, "As soon as you tell someone that you possess humility, you just lost it."

An humble person does not consciously practice humility. He does not get up in the morning and say, "Today I'm going to be humble." Instead, it is a part of his nature brought on by his lifestyle and attitude toward other people.

Unselfishness seems to be the root of humility. Someone who is truly humble is a selfless person, truly esteeming others above himself, wanting the best for others at his own expense, lifting up others instead of himself.

No one can teach humility as a technique. It seems to be an ongoing trait brought about by daily living—seeing the needs of others and responding to those needs.

Someone who is truly humble does not boast or call attention to himself. He is modest in every aspect of his life. Someone with humility does not brag about his own accomplishments but is content to "let another man praise thee, and not thine own mouth; a stranger, and not thine own lips" (Proverbs 27:2).

I knew a man once who was strong yet gentle; a man of few words, yet whose life spoke silently of many accomplishments; a man who truly esteemed others more highly than himself, praising their accomplishments yet never speaking of his own; a man whose exemplary, humble life molded my character. That man was my dad.

Pastors (Shepherds)

A good pastor is not a know-it-all person with a boastful spirit but has a shepherd's heart, full of humility and mercy. His duty is not just a job but a calling from God. "And he gave some . . . pastors" (Ephesians 4:11). God has placed us in a fold with other sheep watched over by a shepherd.

Our pastor's responsibility comes from God, and he is accountable to God for us: "That I may present you . . . to Christ" (II Corinthians 11:2).

God has charged him to love, lead, and "feed the flock" (I Peter 5:2). God also gave him the responsibility to protect the flock, to watch out for potential dangers. He is to reprove, rebuke, and exhort (II Timothy 4:2). Therefore, his duty is not merely to pacify but to challenge and to help us reach maturity: "That ye may grow" (I Peter 2:2).

As we grow, we will learn to love and appreciate "thy rod and thy staff" (Psalm 23:4). Our shepherd with his unpretentious Christ-like spirit was sent by God to guide and lead us to victory. We must pray that we will have a teachable spirit, for this is necessary in order for us to be led.

When God Created Pastors

When the Lord created pastors, the angel looked on with interest. Peering over God's shoulder, the angel asked, "What's that you're stuffing him with?"

God took another scoop and poured it into his creation. Then almost as an afterthought, he added another and another. "That is called Compassion," He answered.

"But, Lord, isn't that too much? Won't people call him a compromiser?"

God smiled and then for good measure added yet another scoop. "It won't be the first time, angel. Don't you remember that in the days of my flesh because I showed compassion on the sinner I, too, was called a compromiser? I want to fashion a pastor in my likeness."

Then the angel nearly had a heart attack. Excitedly, he tugged on God's sleeve. "Lord, do you realize You got carried away and gave him three pairs of eyes? Won't he be considered a freak?"

God worked and smoothed and smiled, content with His creation. "A pastor is sometimes required to see through closed doors, to see things behind his back as well as things before him. A pastor is required to see the unseen, to see pitfalls and obstacles, and to see farther down the road than anyone else."

The angel was silent as God fashioned the ears (large enough to hear many, many confidences), the tongue (small enough not to repeat them), the shoulders (broad enough to bear the burdens of others), the legs (strong enough to run with patience the race), but couldn't contain himself when God fashioned the enormous heart. Bursting with curiosity, he asked, "Lord, why such a large heart?"

With a glow of satisfaction, God positioned the huge heart within the bosom of his pastor. "Good pastors must have an humble shepherd's heart, and a shepherd's heart must be big to contain all a shepherd's attributes. He must be gentle and tender and true, but also righteous and stern and tough."

The angel timidly leaned over and touched the pastor, "Lord, is he durable? Will he wear well? Will he break? What's he made of? Not plastic, I hope."

God smiled. "Don't worry, angel. He's tough! He's made out of good stuff through and through, not merely thin-skinned veneer. He's made to withstand being walked on, kicked about, and stabbed in the back. See how elastic he is? He's made to bounce back!"

God was putting on the finishing touches when the angel squinted, bent down to look more closely, then asked, "Lord, what are those things you have put in his hands?"

God was sober as he answered, "My rod and My staff. A pastor must be a shepherd and a good shepherd delights in his flock—delights in seeing that they are well-fed, safe, and flourishing under his care. It is a comfort and consolation to his sheep to see the rod and the staff in the shepherd's hands. The rod is an instrument of protection to drive off predators. I have placed My rod in the shepherd's hands. It is an extension of My mind—it implies authority. The Scriptures are an extension of My mind, will, and intentions. Therefore, the rod in the hands of the shepherd is a symbol of the Holy Scripture."

The angel knelt down and with reverence gently touched the rod, then the staff. "What about the staff, Lord? This long stick with the funny-looking crook on the end."

God picked up the staff and adjusted the crook. "The rod conveys the concept of authority, of defense against danger, whereas the staff speaks of all that is longsuffering, comforting, and kind.

"The staff is used to draw sheep together in the fold for communion with one another. It is used to draw sheep close to the shepherd. The staff is useful for the shy and timid sheep that normally tend to keep a distance from the shepherd. The staff is also used for guiding sheep into new and unknown paths. It is used to rescue sheep who fall and those who slip under fences.

"Just as I have given the rod as a symbol of the Holy Scriptures, I have given the staff as a symbol of the Holy Spirit. It is the shepherd's task to use the rod (Scriptures) and the staff (Spirit) to protect, feed, and guide his flock."

"Lord," the angel ventured hopefully, "looks like he should have a fairly easy job, don't you think so?"

The Lord groaned. "Alas! It seems that even though the shepherd feeds his sheep and protects them against predators there are sometimes in the flock the 'fence crawlers'—those who are not content with their side of the fence. The grass is greener (to them) on the other side. They are restless and discontented, wanting the best of two worlds.

"It seems that no matter what field or pasture the shepherd feeds his flock, discontented sheep will search all along the fences looking for a loophole to crawl through to the other side. It is not that they lack good pasture. It is simply an ingrained habit—never content with things as they are.

"Often when they force themselves through some such spot in a fence, they end up feeding on bare, brown, burned-up, or inferior pasture. But they never learn their lesson and continue to fence-crawl. Sheep of this nature produce more problems for the shepherd than almost all the rest of the flock combined. It would be bad enough if they were the only ones who did this, but sheep with this nature tend to want to teach others the same tricks, leading them through the same holes and over the same dangerous paths.

"The shepherd must use his rod and his staff to try to save all the flock, even the restless and discontented. But, sometimes, in spite of all he can do to give the best care, they still want something else. At this point, to save the rest of the flock, as the discontented slip through the fence that last time, with sadness he lets them go."

With an aching heart, the angel was sober as God bent down and gently added the final ingredient—the tears, dripping from His own eyes.

"Blessed are the poor in spirit: for theirs is the kingdom of heaven."

Summary

True or False

1. One of the definitions of humility is "to be inconspicuous."

2. It is human nature to be humble.

3. Humility seems to be an ongoing trait brought about by daily seeing the needs of others and responding to those needs.

4. Someone who is boastful and a know-it-all recognizes the vast gulf between God and himself.

5. Someone with humility brags about his own accomplishments and knowledge.

6. When you tell someone you possess humility, you have just lost it.

7. Self-righteousness is a trait signifying a humble person.

8. A pastor's responsibility comes from those who elected him and he is accountable only to them.

9. The pastor who possesses a shepherd's heart is full of Christ-like humility and mercy.

10. The rod as well as the staff in the hands of our shepherd will guide us to victory.

Answers

1. True, 2. False, 3. True, 4. False, 5. False, 6. True, 7. False, 8. False, 9. True, 10.True

3

Running from Pain or Comforted by God

The world's version:
"Blessed are those who run from pain, seeking to make life simply fun and games."

Jesus' version:
"Blessed are they that mourn: for they shall be comforted."

Feeling inadequate in the face of life-changing events, many people refuse to face facts. Shrinking from reality by refusing to find solutions to life's problems is a form of escapism. By not facing fears, we doom ourselves to be imprisoned by them.

Some people attempt to drown reality in a whirl of escaping anything that might cause any pain. Living this way, a person constantly seeks to make life simply fun and games. We cannot solve the deep problems of life by pushing them aside, however. When we face reality, we begin to find ways to accept the difficult times of our life and move on.

When Life Isn't Fair

The wind rose to a sudden shriek and there was a splintering crash as a branch snapped from a tree. I was driving north, the headlights of the little Nissan gnawing holes in the darkness. Jagged crooks of lightning rent the unfriendly sky, lighting up the roadway ahead and the tree branch directly in my path.

Bringing the car to a halt a few feet from the blockage, I suddenly began trembling while tears of self-pity gushed unchecked. What was I doing here? Why couldn't I be at home, snug and safe?

This past year had not been easy. I was walking a path I had not been before, treading on unfamiliar turf. With widowhood had come a yearning for all I had lost. I wanted to run away from new responsibilities. The new responsibilities included the second job that I was trying to get to in the midst of the storm. With widowhood had also come the awareness of reduced income and the necessity of survival.

I had just enough time between my regular job in Kilgore at the county tax office and my second job in Longview in the credit office of Dillard's Department Store to drive the twenty miles it took to get there, but now the downed tree would make me late.

Surveying the blocked roadway, I gripped the steering wheel, backed up, pulled forward, and backed again until I had turned the little Nissan around and started back the way I had come. Veering off blocked Highway 42 onto Interstate 20, I wiped away the tears and sped toward my job in Longview thinking about life's ups and downs—when life seemingly isn't fair.

Struggles and Growth

What do we do when life seems to tumble in? We have dared to dream big dreams. We have made great commitments and we are determined never to give up. Then it happens! Our world starts coming apart. What do we do now?

Surprisingly, there is no growth without pain, struggle, separation. The eagle throws her little ones out of her nest so that the young will learn to fly. A child has to leave the crib and eventually the security of the home as he goes out into the world. A person who has been protected from all conflict will never become a well-adjusted human being. We only grow through struggle and difficulty.

How, then, does one grow into an emotionally whole person? How does the heart grow? By experiencing laughter and tears. By tasting hope and disappointment. By tasting success and failure. By picking ourselves up and daring to dream again. This is the growth process that turns us into mature people.

Personality is not something that is fixed. It continually grows and develops. As it grows, it can be guided, improved, and strengthened. A person with a well-developed personality grows with each new experience, whether happy or sad, and makes it a part of himself. A person with a well-adjusted personality has a definite code by which he lives and is in little danger of acting against the principles in which he believes no matter what obstacle or adverse situation may present itself.

Courage to Change

Being confronted with painful events of life, we often find ourselves in stressful situations. Events themselves aren't stressful; it's how we perceive them and our attitude toward them that makes us feel tense. For some people, a roller-coaster ride is stressful; for others it's a thrilling experience.

In general, stress comes from feeling out of control of our own life. Others seem to be in control, not we ourselves. We feel trapped in situations of life. The key to relieving stress when we think life isn't fair is gaining control over situations we have the power to change and accepting those we don't. There is a lot of truth in the serenity prayer recited at Alcoholics Anonymous meetings: "God grant me the courage to change what I can, the strength to accept what I can't, and the wisdom to know the difference."

Therein lies our problem—not having the wisdom to know the difference. We worry, become agitated, and fret over situations beyond our control to change (such as death of a loved one, terminal illness, divorce, job layoffs, and so on) instead of finding ways to accept those unchangeable situations by daring to change those things within our power to change. We have the power to change our attitude, and more than likely, when we do we will be an overcomer. It is amazing what people have accomplished who have dared to try.

Some think about changing the circumstances in which they find themselves but concentrate on the difficulties instead of the possibilities until their chance is gone. Opportunity is like a vapor: it vanishes quickly. Usually it is the anticipation of failure rather than failure itself that paralyzes us. When our world tumbles in, it is the ability to accept the challenge of change that will eventually bring joy.

The Tempering Fires of Change

Coming to terms with the death of a loved one, divorce, illness, or loss of a job is always painful. Some try to run from that pain by fleeing reality, refusing to accept an unchangeable situation. But faith reminds us that there can be a design for our lives that we may not fully grasp. In the Old Testament, Job suffered repeated personal calamities yet steadfastly refused to turn against God. When Job's trials ended at last, his faith was rewarded. Similarly, individuals in crisis often share a sense of being tested, the purposes and rewards of which are revealed only much later—if ever.

I remember that I once worried a lot about little things. But after my husband, Cecil, died, I learned a lot about life and fear. I realized that once I had overcome the trauma of his death, I could handle anything.

Not everyone benefits from every crisis, but many who go through the tempering fires of change successfully emerge better prepared to meet whatever challenges come their way.

The Tempering Fires of God

One cold, rainy night in winter, I sat curled up on the couch lazily watching the fire in the fireplace as it burned down to beautiful red-hot, glowing coals. Keith threw on another log and in a matter of minutes the fire was licking hungrily around the new log from the red, glowing bed of coals and fast consuming it.

Watching Keith, my heart stirred within me as I remembered the tempering fires of change we both had endured. Keith had struggled through the changes involved when his wife, Nadine, succumbed to cancer and when his daughter, Linda Jo, died of the same disease at the young age of thirty-eight.

I, too, had been put through the tempering fires of change when my husband, Cecil Camp, died suddenly from a ruptured abdominal aneurysm. After five years of widowhood, my life changed again when God brought Keith into my life and we married.

When the fire died again, Keith threw on another log. This time I watched with interest as the coals sputtered and spewed, smoked and smoldered, but never burst into flame as before.

When Keith added some twigs and splinters (kindling, he said) the fire soon blazed again. Answering my unspoken questions, he explained, "The first log was seasoned (dry wood) but the second was freshly cut wood (green)."

Musing, I thought, There is nothing wrong with the fire; it is always the same. But the way it burns depends upon the condition of the fuel put on it. Similarly, the condition of the heart of the individual person determines what extent and what effect the tempering fires of the Spirit of God have in his life. The same fire that hardens clay can also melt wax. The same fire that purifies can also consume. The same fire that separates pure gold from its alloy leaves stone intact. The same fire, but the end result depends upon the fuel.

When our world tumbles in and God sees fit to change the circumstances of our lives entirely, the tempering fires of the Spirit of God in a person's life will either harden his heart in bitterness and rebellion as it did to Pharaoh's or melt his heart in acceptance and repentance as it did to the apostle Paul's. The same tempering fire that extracts the goodness and mercy from one person's character leaves another's heart unmoved and untouched. The same fire, but different results.

As I watched the fire in the fireplace, I thought of the three conditions that must exist before a fire can be made:

1. There must be fuel, a substance that will burn.
2. The fuel must be raised to its kindling temperature.
3. There must be plenty of oxygen (usually taken from the air).

Kindling temperature, or kindling point, is the amount of heat needed to make a substance burst into flame. Every burnable substance has its own kindling temperature. The lower the kindling temperature the more easily a substance will catch fire. Some materials, such as paper or dry wood, have a low kindling temperature. For paper it is 363° F, while wood requires 469-516° F, so we can easily set fire to them. Others, such as coal or coke, have a high kindling temperature and are difficult to ignite. And still others, such as stone, will not burn.

"Lord," I prayed, "when stressful situations develop in my life, help me not be difficult for the Spirit to ignite, and by all means help me not to have a stony, rebellious heart. I want to be like the dry wood Keith threw on the fire—seasoned, tempered, and easy to ignite."

The Word of God has been called the breath (oxygen) of life. When we continually surround ourselves with the Word—studying, listening, and obeying God—we draw spiritual oxygen to the fire of the Spirit within, allowing Him to work in us and through us, molding our lives, changing us to His perfect will. Just like the rushing mighty wind, perhaps symbolizing the breath of God, that kindled the flames of that first outpouring on the Day of

Pentecost, God's Word kindles the flame of the Spirit in us.

The prophet felt the Spirit as a flame in his heart; he described it as a "burning fire shut up in my bones" (Jeremiah 20:9). As the two disciples on the Emmaus road listened to the teaching of Jesus, they felt the presence of the Spirit and thereby recognized Jesus. "Did not our heart burn within us while he talked with us by the way, and while he opened to us, the scriptures?" (Luke 24:32).

Years ago in my high school science classes we studied about a substance known as phosphorous. It has such a low kindling point that it will start burning in the air at normal room temperature. Indeed, it must be placed under water in order to keep from burning.

In being sensitive to God's presence, God's people should strive to be like phosphorous—having a kindling point so low that they start "burning" even during the normal activities of daily living. When circumstances bring trials, hardships, illness, or financial woes, God's Spirit will purge our spirits, burning out the dross, and turn these adversities into a testimony of His grace, presence, and power in us.

The name of phosphorous comes from Greek words that mean "light bearer," because in one of its forms it will glow in the dark. It glows when exposed to air. In like manner, when God's people are exposed to God's Word, it makes them glow with God's glory. We are His light bearers to people in this dark world of sin. God uses us to show them the way to righteousness, peace, and joy—to show them that in the midst of adversity there is hope.

Life's Ups and Downs

Learning from changes in life is the mark of a mature

Christian. We must realize that with each turning point there are new possibilities for reaching a deeper commitment. Disappointment and shattered dreams come to us all, but our reaction to these things determines our future. How do we react? Bitterly? Rebelliously? If so, we will feel a million miles from God. We will feel all alone and ask many times, "Does God care?"

To be sure, when life isn't fair, God is. A loving father, He is preparing us and shaping us for what is to come. Our attitude toward life's experiences determines whether or not we have fear or faith.

The very trials that test our faith most severely and make it seem that God has forsaken us can lead us closer to Christ that we may lay all our burdens at His feet and experience the peace that He gives us in exchange.

Lesson of the Tapestry

A tapestry is a fabric woven with yarns of different colors to form a picture or an ornamental design. Craftsmen make tapestries by weaving the design into the fabric itself, winding the weft or woof (horizontal) threads around the warp (vertical) threads. They press the stitches tightly against each other so that the colored woof yarns entirely cover the undyed warp yarns. Unlike the rug weaver, the tapestry weaver faces the back of the fabric as he works.

The back of a tapestry is as beautiful and intricately woven as the front. From the back, the pattern is not as discernible, but the colors and needlework are as beautiful. God works unseen in the background of our life, weaving the final tapestry that is seen. We can't see the beautiful result because we are looking at the back side (immediate heartaches) of our experiences. But if we turn them around and realize that God makes no mistakes, then the experiences that are woven into the tapestry of our life will take on new meaning, and the end result will show the beautiful pattern that God intended.

The Survivor

Early every evening I'd stand gazing out the window at my husband, Keith Clark, as he left with the three dogs, Prissy, Missy, and Skippy, for their nightly romp in the back woods of our sixty-one-acre farm. I always felt as though my love ran down the path and padded along beside him while the dogs happily flushed out an elusive rabbit or squirrel. We had been married less than two years.

When we first met I thought I might be imagining that we were falling in love. But it wasn't my imagination at all. It was love. Keith was sixty-seven when we became acquainted and I was sixty-one. We'd both lost our mates—his of forty-six years and mine of thirty-eight years. He had also suffered the loss of a daughter, only thirty-eight years old. I had been a widow for five years when we married and had struggled through my own horrendous process of grieving. For some people grief takes longer to heal than it does for others. Keith's wife, Nadine, had been dead less than a year when we married; his daughter, Linda Jo, only two years. Sometimes when Keith came in from the woods, he looked pained, sad. But he'd give me a quick smile. I'd search his gentle face, wondering what might be beneath the sometimes not believable smile.

After his scampers with the dogs in the woods, Keith

liked to come in and tell me about the progress of a tiny wren that had built its nest in one of his boots that hung on a nail in the old shed at the back of our property.

"She has three beautiful eggs, baby."

Then, "The baby birds are hatched out now, sweetheart."

"The little wren knows me, honey, and talks to me," Keith said one day. "I want you to come and see her."

So I went. At the sound of his voice calling, "Hey, girl!" the tiny wren came flapping her wings excitedly and circled his head.

"Chirp! Chirp! Chirp!"

He lifted me up to the nest so I could see the three tiny balls of fluff waiting with open-mouthed expectancy.

Each evening after that when Keith came in from his walk in the woods, I'd ask, "What did the little wren say today?" Once, he told me, "She said, 'See how fast my babies are growing? Soon they will be flapping out of the nest!' "

One evening I heard Keith calling my name over and over as he came in. Something was drastically wrong. I ran into the living room. He sat in his recliner, bent over, his head in his hands. He was crying. He didn't make any effort to hide his tears. That's one of the things I love about my husband. He doesn't run into the bathroom when he cries. I knelt before him, waiting.

"They're dead!"

Who? I wondered. Who is dead? Neighbors? Family? Talk to me, Keith!

Finally, he looked directly into my eyes and spoke softly, haltingly. "All three of the baby birds . . . are dead." I looked into a face filled with fresh grief without restraint. "Apparently, they were trying to fly. They all three fell into the dogs' bucket of drinking water and drowned. They're just lying there in a pile of feathers. The mother bird is flying around in circles, hollering."

I wasn't sure what to do, so I waited. After a few moments Keith stood up and said, "I must bury the birds. The mother doesn't understand why her babies won't get up and fly."

I stood up too and watched him walk to the garage. He picked up a shovel. Without my shoes and without any knowledge of how to comfort my husband, I followed him, feeling almost like an intruder. I touched his shoulder so gently he could easily have ignored it. "Would it be okay if I go along?" I wondered, Why am I whispering?

"Yes, I want you to go," he said immediately.

Lord, I don't know how to help him or even why I'm going, I thought. Please help me. I ran to get my shoes and threw on a jacket. Together we set out for the grim task.

We heard the survivor's screams before we reached the shed. As Keith dug silently in the sandy Texas soil, I sat close to him on the ground, my arms encircling my knees. Rather than look at Keith or the three mounds of feathers, I stared at the new moon rising and tried very hard to concentrate on its beauty—but the bird's panicky calls disturbed any attempts at serenity. The lone bird circled near to where Keith dug.

"Chirp! Chirp! Chirp!" she wailed. I guess she thought that Keith could somehow make everything okay again.

I felt like saying, "Look, bird, it's over. You must accept death and pain. I know because I've lived through it. All this hollering isn't going to help." But the bird had never "talked" to me so I remained quiet, still uncertain of my role in this unusual drama.

Keith kept his eyes on the grave as he dug and started talking to the surviving bird, softly, without ever looking up. She appeared to listen intently as she perched on a fence post only inches away.

"I know it hurts, girl. I understand. Really, I do. Life isn't fair. I'm so sorry, girl."

"Chirp. Chirp. Chirp. Chirp . . . "

I tightened my arms about my knees and looked up at the incredibly beautiful moon, thinking, You have to endure it, bird. You have no choice when you are—left. Something akin to agony stirred within me briefly and tears suddenly stung my eyes. To be left—the horror of being left!

Keith placed an enormous rock on the grave and we stood looking down at it for what seemed like a long time. As we turned and walked away the lone bird shrieked at us. Then she flapped her wings and flew slowly, without purpose, into the old shed. The picture stuck in my mind. She thought she had no real reason to live.

The next morning Keith went out before I was awake. I was sitting at the kitchen table drinking coffee when he came in, excitement in his voice, "Come on, baby!"

"Where to?" I asked.

"Just come on."

So once again scrambling for my shoes I followed Keith to the old shed. The grieving bird was nowhere in sight but we heard her lonesome wails. Keith cupped his hands to his mouth and called, "Here, girl!"

Then silently Keith nudged me and pointed to a nearby tree. "What is it?" I asked.

"Watch," he said.

As the grieving bird came chirping desperately in response to Keith's calls, out of the tree to meet her came another bird. "Her mate," Keith explained.

The calls of the grieving bird changed unmistakably to ones of possible hope. "Chirp? Chirp? Chirp?"

She approached the newcomer excitedly and they blended together, touching their bills lightly again and again almost as though they were kissing. Then she began to swoop over our heads, dipping and flapping her wings ecstatically.

"Oh, happy day! I was so terrified! I thought I'd be alone forever." Amazingly, I was learning to understand bird talk!

Keith reached out and pulled me to him. Tight and close. In fact, I had never felt quite so close to him, or so needed. "Let's go home," he said. We walked past the grave with the stone marker and up the hill with our arms around each other.

"Blessed are they that mourn: for they shall be comforted."

Summary

True or False

1. Shrinking from reality by refusing to find solutions to life's problems is a form of escapism.
2. By not facing fears, we doom ourselves to be imprisoned by them.
3. Personality is fixed; it cannot be developed, guided, improved, or strengthened.
4. Stress comes from feeling out of control of our own life.
5. We do not have the power to change our attitude.
6. We should accept every situation as unchangeable instead of daring to change those things within our power to change.
7. The condition of the heart of the individual determines what extent and what effect the tempering fires of the Spirit of God have in his life.
8. The same fire that separates pure gold from its alloy leaves stone intact. The same fire, but the end result depends upon the fuel.
9. When our world tumbles in and God sees fit to change the circumstances of our lives entirely, the tempering fires of the Spirit of God in a person's life will either harden his heart in bitterness and rebellion or melt his heart in acceptance and repentance.
10. The very trials that test our faith most severely are really letting us know that God has forsaken us.

Answers

1. True, 2. True, 3. False, 4. True, 5. False, 6. False, 7. True, 8. True, 9. True, 10. False

4

Self-Centeredness or Meekness

The world's version:
"Blessed are the egotistical, vain and self-centered: for they shall view the world from their lofty perch."

Jesus' version:
"Blessed are the meek: for they shall inherit the earth."

Selfishness and self-centeredness are prevalent in our world today. They indicate a lack of spiritual values. Real Christian love is not selfish, nor is it self-centered. The motivating factor of Christian love is a genuine concern for others, the desire to be constantly aware of what God wants.

By contrast, Jezebel was a vain, self-centered queen—a patroness of idolatry, a murderess, and a woman who incited her husband to evil. She was always thinking of self: self-gratification, self-glory, self-exaltation.

If Queen Jezebel could be given a reprieve, perhaps this is what she would say to our generation:

"Oh! What a relief to be out of that inferno! Why am I here? Oh, now I remember. I was told that I was being given a short reprieve from the regions of hell to speak to this generation. But what could I possibly say that would be relevant to your day and time?

"Oh, how well I remember that day on Mt. Carmel. I was never so humiliated in my life when my husband, King Ahab, told me what Elijah had done. He made Ahab a laughingstock in front of all his subjects!

"The nerve of Elijah, belittling Baal and calling fire down from heaven and claiming it was from the only true God—the God of Israel. Do you blame me for threatening Elijah for humiliating me? You probably would have done the same."

(There it is again, Jezebel—self. Retaliating. Meekness never retaliates but self always does.)

"But all of this is ancient history. It couldn't possibly apply to your day. Or could it? Do you retaliate when self is not glorified or exalted? Do you swell up in your own little world when things do not go your way?

"As it was with me, there are many people in your day who worship other gods. Oh, I don't mean that nowadays you make little gods out of wood or stone and bow down to them. The gods I refer to are more subtle than that, having to do with the spirit within mankind. As with me, the god you worship most is called self. The god of self comes wrapped in many guises, such as self-glory and self-exaltation, but never self-denial, meekness, or submissiveness.

"I was thinking only of self that day Naboth wouldn't sell his vineyard to Ahab. 'No way!' Naboth said. 'It's been in my family for years. I won't sell at any price!' You know the story—how I took it in my hands to have Naboth killed so we could take possession of his vineyard (I Kings 21).

"How I laughed the day Elijah said I would die a horrible death! Me, Queen Jezebel? He said after the dogs got through with me there wouldn't be anything left to bury. What a laugh! His prophecy didn't come to pass, at least not right away, and I laughed even harder. But as with every true prophecy of God, it did come to pass—in God's timing. Every Jezebel will come to the same end. Judgment always comes to those who connive, deceive, and destroy.

"If only I had my life to live over it might be different. Perhaps babies would actually be named after me. Think about it. How many babies have you ever heard named Jezebel? That should tell you how wicked and self-centered I was! If I had my life to live over, history would call me the good Queen Jezebel instead of the wicked Queen Jezebel. Instead of causing another person pain and death by stealing his inheritance and instead of belittling the man of God, I would learn how to possess myself with a meek and submissive spirit. Oh, that I could call back the past and relive my life!"

Meekness and Submissiveness

It was Shakespeare who said, "Call back yesterday, bid time return!" Jezebel cannot bid time return. What she sowed in life, she reaped in death. Jezebel, possessor of a proud, haughty spirit, is the direct opposite of someone possessing a meek and submissive spirit. Jesus Christ is the most influential man who ever lived, yet He possessed a meek and submissive spirit. "I am meek and lowly," He told us (Matthew 11:29).

Many people are confused about the meaning of meekness. Sometimes they side-step this self-description of Jesus because they view meekness as weakness and spinelessness. Some people have conjured up in their mind that meekness means a mealy-mouthed individual who conforms to the crowd—one with no opinion of his own but one who vacillates between opinions according to whichever group he is with. But that is far, far from what Jesus meant when He referred to Himself as meek.

Strength under Control

Praos is the Greek word rendered as meek. It speaks of strength under control. It is the term used of taming a wild horse, a stallion that has been in the field all its life, is brought into the pen, and then broken until it is under control. It is still strong, still muscular, but controlled and tame. Its strength is under control. It has become meek.

A meek man is not weak and spineless. He is strong, but his strength is under control, the control of God. A meek person is obedient to the will of God.

In the Gospels Jesus said, "I came down from heaven, not to do mine own will, but the will of him that sent me" (John 6:38). Jesus was obedient to the Father. He was under submission to authority. Meekness will automatically bring obedience. If we are God-controlled, we are obedient.

Jesus said He could have called more than twelve legions of angels to rescue Him and to circumvent the cross (Matthew 26:53). Being God manifest in the flesh, He had the ability to summon the mighty heavenly host, yet He was obedient and submissive to the will of the Father. His strength was under control. His human will was in submission to the will of the Spirit. He was meek.

I can see Michael and Gabriel poised, flaming swords

drawn, ready to lead the mighty heavenly host to swoop Him up and carry Him back to His rightful place in glory. I can see Michael and Gabriel as they fidgeted, waiting for just the flick of an eyelash that would summon them. But the flick of an eyelash did not come, only the words, "It is finished," wafting their way upward to the waiting army. Jesus was obedient, even to death. He was meek.

Moses was "very meek" (Numbers 12:3). Never did anyone ever accuse Moses of being weak. But once he was an uncontrolled, hot-tempered man. Then we read how God took hold of him and made him a leader of the children of Israel. His strength was under the control of God and he became a God-controlled man, one whom God could use. Therefore, the Bible calls him meek. God cannot use us until we become meek—God-controlled. Hot-blooded Saul of Tarsus was changed into the greatest missionary Christianity has ever known. God took his zeal and channeled it in another direction, one that He could use.

On the other hand, there are people with a naturally shy, retiring, or timid nature. They are naturally gentle. But we must not confuse a soft-spoken voice with meekness. In order to be used of God this type of individual must also become meek.

How can a person with a shy and gentle nature become any more meek? Just as a person with a strong, outgoing personality must be broken so that he is God-controlled, the person with a timid nature must also be broken so that he is God-controlled. Sometimes behind a soft-spoken voice lies a stubborn will. God breaks that person's timid nature and gives him a holy boldness to work for Him.

In school, I was naturally timid and shy. I hated having to stand before the class and give an oral book report. If I knew beforehand about the book report, I would manage to be sick that day. It wasn't that I didn't know the material; it was just that I was too timid to stand before the class and talk. But when God came into my life, He changed my nature. He gave me a holy boldness and a desire to communicate with others about His goodness. He gave me a new nature, one that He could use.

King of Beasts: Meek

The lion tamer has so broken the will of the king of the beasts that he is as docile as a kitten. He has become meek. He is still strong, still able to kill the lion tamer with just a flick of his paw, but his strength is under control—the control of his master. He has become meek. Not weak and spineless, but controlled.

Black Jack: Meek

When my nephew, Trey, was a teenager he had a black Labrador retriever named Black Jack. Trey taught the dog an amazing trick. He placed a dog biscuit on the dog's nose and trained him to sit with it there until given the command, "Eat." I have watched the dog sit for many, many minutes, perhaps an hour, with the biscuit on his nose. Then Trey would give the command, "Eat!" and with the flick of his nose Black Jack would toss the dog biscuit into the air, catch it in his mouth, and eat it. Black Jack was under the control of his master. He was a big, strong dog that had become meek, not weak. His own will was submissive to his master's will.

Skippy: Meek

On the other hand, our dog Skippy came to us with a

shy, retiring nature but in the process of time learned boldness. An abandoned, half-starved, pint-sized dog, Skippy clung pathetically to Keith when he first found her and brought her home. She cowered at his feet day and night, never leaving his side. Only by much love, coaxing, and training was her timid nature broken.

Now, Skippy's greatest joy is to run free with the other dogs, Prissy and Missy, on the sixty-one-acre farm, chasing squirrels through the piney woods, swimming in Little Cypress Bayou, and learning all about deer, raccoons, rabbits, and possums.

Skippy is now the self-proclaimed caretaker of the home; her bark will prohibit people from entering until they are welcomed to come in. I don't know if she understands people talk or not, but she will cock her head, prick up her ears, and obediently trot off down the lane to apprehend an invisible burglar when told to do so.

Skippy delighted everyone by learning to run up the leaning, dead tree trunk in the back yard pretending to be a cat while sitting for hours guarding the hole at the top, hoping to nab some unsuspecting varmint.

With one ear to the ground, Skippy the clown traps a mole by walking on tiptoe until she locates the little scamp, then thrusts her head into his hole, drags him out, and triumphantly deposits him at Keith's feet.

Spurred on by this hunter instinct, Skippy's nocturnal prowlings invariably end with her incessant barking when she corners a possum in the bushes. Skippy's never-ending barking is Keith's signal to jump out of bed and run out into the night armed with a .22 rifle and flashlight. Gripping the flashlight between his teeth, Keith shines the light into the bushes, fires the gun, and the nightly ritual ends as Skippy happily snatches up her treasured possum and trots off.

We laughed when the tables were turned on Skippy one day. Dashing to the front yard at the sound of Keith's rifle, Skippy pounced on the varmint that plopped to the ground from the low-lying limb of the oak tree. With her tail between her legs, Skippy ran out of the yard yelping when she discovered the varmint that Keith had shot in the tree was not a play toy of a possum but a big, black snake.

Skippy's story is a provoking testimony to her changed nature. No longer timid and cowering, her greatest joy is to please her master by protecting his home from intruders and by trapping the many varmint intruders of the farm, then happily depositing them at Keith's feet (all except the snake).

In her boldness, Skippy has become meek—not aggressive and domineering, but meek and obedient because she seeks to please her master.

Conformed to the Image of Christ

When the Bible speaks of our conforming to the image of Christ, it simply means that God wants to take our stallion nature (our natural tendencies) and break it so that we come out gentle and meek. Not weak, not spineless, but useful and valuable.

Several qualities characterize a person whose natural nature has been broken by God:

1. He is approachable—easy to have contact with, talk to, and ask questions of.

2. He is sensitive and alert to his environment. Open to the opinions of others, he welcomes instructions.

3. His actions are thoughtful, and he does not inconsiderately hurt others' feelings.

4. He has a corporate awareness, being sensitive to the needs of the church body and to others.

Who are the meek of this world? The meek are not the mealy-mouthed wimps but the strong who are controlled by God. They are the builders who strive to bring this world in line with God's plan. They repair the damage done by self-centered, reckless people whose strength is not controlled.

The future does not belong to those who ruin everything they touch; it belongs to the builders, to those who are controlled and directed by God.

"Blessed are the meek: for they shall inherit the earth."

Summary

True or False

1. The motivating factor of Christian love is selfishness and self-centeredness.
2. One of the traits of meekness is retaliation.
3. A proud, haughty spirit is the direct opposite of a meek and submissive spirit.
4. Someone who is meek is a spineless, mealy-mouthed wimp that conforms to the crowd, someone with no opinion of his own but one who vacillates between opinions according to whichever group he is with.
5. A meek person is a strong person whose strength is under control, the control of God.
6. Meekness will automatically bring obedience to God.
7. Someone who has a soft-spoken voice and is naturally gentle should automatically be considered meek.
8. Sometimes behind a soft-spoken voice lies a stubborn will.
9. Someone with a naturally shy, timid nature must also be broken so that he is God-controlled.
10. Someone whose nature has been broken by God until he has become meek is (1) approachable; (2) sensitive, alert, and open to the opinions of others; and (3) considerate of the needs and feelings of others.

Answers

1. False, 2. False, 3. True, 4. False, 5. True, 6. True, 7. False, 8. True, 9. True, 10. True

5

Applause of the World or Applause of God

The world's version:
"Blessed are those who ignore God's laws: for they shall receive the applause of the world."

Jesus' version:
"Blessed are they which do hunger and thirst after righteousness: for they shall be filled."

Everyone must obey God's natural law of gravity or suffer devastation. If we jump out of an airplane without a parachute because we do not believe the law applies to us, we will quickly reap the consequences. Few people ignore the law of gravity, but many ignore God's spiritual laws of morality.

The superstars who epitomize immorality are in the limelight and have the applause of the world. Young people pattern their lives after the heroes of the day, striving to imitate their hair, clothes, and lifestyle. Crime, violence, immorality, and suicide run rampant in their wake.

Moral and spiritual laws are trampled. Parents are frustrated; teachers outraged.

To those who ignore God's laws, having the applause of the world means more than living a life pleasing to God. Trampling God's laws, fathers desert their families in search of fame and fortune. Shedding undramatic and routine lives, mothers abandon toddlers in search of glamour and fantasy. The desire for the limelight, glory, and attention only feeds a person's ego rather than making God the center of his living. It is the hidden things in our private life and not the showy moments of public acclaim that test our character. Walking in obedience when we are all alone is more important than displaying our talents before crowds, and obedience is more important even than offering a sacrifice to God (I Samuel 15:22).

Some in today's generation ridicule those who still adhere to the sanctity of marriage and the home. Today's superstars, in their music and in their very lifestyle, glamorize immorality and trample underfoot the laws of God.

Marriage means commitment, and this group laughs at such an old-fashioned view while encouraging and even demanding promiscuity. Unwed mothers and absent fathers follow in their wake and are the norm for children born into this type of situation.

On the other hand, rather than the applause of the world, a Christian home receives the applause of God.

The Christian Home

There has been much talk from politicians and others about family values. They seem to mean one thing to one group and another to another group. But to the Christian, family values mean establishing and maintaining a home centered around Christ and His teachings. The moral as well as the spiritual teachings of Christ should be the foundation of every Christian home. Striving to instill these family values into our children should be the very essence of our existence.

Marriage

Every home begins with two people who commit themselves to be faithful to the other in all situations of life, "in sickness and in health . . . for richer, for poorer . . . " But the Christian home adds the third ingredient—Christ. A Christian marriage takes three.

Oneness of Purpose

If both parties in a marriage serve the Lord with all their hearts, the probability of success in their marriage is exceedingly high. To attain the highest meaning of marriage there must be oneness of spiritual purpose in addition to physical attraction and complementary natures. Both must be fully committed to the Lord. Such a marriage has a solid foundation, for the two parties have a strong bond of unity before God.

In a marriage having oneness of purpose, there is no striving as to who gives orders and who obeys. Christ is the head who is to be obeyed. And if Christ is obeyed, then His Word is obeyed, and husband and wife find their rightful positions. There is no struggling for power. (See Ephesians 5:22-25; Colossians 3:18-19; I Peter 3:1-7.)

Close Your Eyes

"Open your eyes!"

Many parents have said this to a son or daughter

contemplating marriage. True, before marriage is the time to open one's eyes wide to possible difficulties. But after marriage, the first thing to learn is to close our eyes. We discover enough weaknesses in our counterpart without looking. How many more difficulties there will be if we seek them on purpose!

Whatever the type of person we marry, we must expect to live with that for life. We must not look for difficulties and weaknesses with a view toward changing them. For a marriage to be a success, the husband and wife must be blind and deaf to the weaknesses of the other.

Be Willing to Adjust

One basic condition that marriage implies is sacrifice. No matter how much alike the dispositions of the couple are, sooner or later they will discover lots of differences. To have a harmonious home, the husband and wife must learn to adjust, adapt, and accommodate the other.

Learn to find out the likes, dislikes, thoughts, and viewpoints of your counterpart. As much as possible, sacrifice your own feeling, opinion, and viewpoint. In this way, family problems will greatly diminish. To insist dogmatically on your own viewpoint at all times will not result in a happy home. Giving in at times to the likes and dislikes of the other is not a weakness but a strength. Only someone with strong character can lay aside his own opinion and accept the other's view.

Be Appreciative

Learn to see the strengths, the virtues, the beauty of the other. Learn to express your appreciation to the other.

If there is no expression of appreciation, misunderstandings and problems will arise. It may seem a small thing for a husband to thank his wife for a good meal, yet when he does so, she realizes her efforts to please him have not gone unnoticed. Likewise, a husband will stand a little taller when his wife lets him know how much she appreciates his hard work to earn a living for the family. The success or failure of a marriage depends much on appreciation and acknowledgment of each other's strengths and virtues, as well as on restraint from noticing each other's weaknesses and faults.

Parenthood

The goal of a Christian home is to help children grow into adulthood with godly values and balanced lives. According to Scripture, the father's responsibility toward his family is that of leader, provider, and protector, while the mother's responsibility includes that of helper, home manager, and teacher.

A Double Standard

A child is a trust. His moral standard comes from his parents' moral standard. To lead our children to God, we must ourselves walk with God. The reason for the failure of many Christian families is that the parents expect their children to be better than they are. They expect their children not to love the world while they themselves love the world. We cannot set a standard for our children and not live by it ourselves. The standard we follow in spiritual things will eventually be the standard of our children. Children tend to pattern their lives after their parents, either consciously or subconsciously. For this reason, parents must truly walk with God.

Empty Promises

We must never make an empty promise. If children discover a lack of trustworthiness in their parents' words, they themselves will be careless when they grow up. They will surmise that they can say and do things thoughtlessly.

Discipline Wisely

Shakespeare said, "It is a wise father that knows his own child." The way we enforce our words with our children depends upon the individual child. Each child is different, and the parent must choose wisely the disciplinary action to take. What works with one will not work with another. For this reason, a wise parent will seek to know his child.

Be an Encourager

When children do well, parents should show proper appreciation. It is sad that some parents seem to know only how to scold. This easily provokes children and discourages even those who really have a desire to be good. Paul told us not to do this (Colossians 3:21).

We should build up a child's self-esteem by encouraging him. An unwanted and unloved child can sense being a burden and will grow up to feel worthless and unloved. On the other hand, a loved and appreciated child will grow up with a feeling of security knowing that he is a worthwhile human being. Children should be encouraged and rewarded as well as disciplined.

Be of One Mind

For a family to be solid, the Christian father and mother must be of one mind. They must agree. Often a father and mother provide an opening for their children to rebel because they themselves do not stand together. It is difficult for the children to follow a definite standard of conduct if the parents do not agree. If the father says yes and the mother says no (or vice versa), the children will ask whoever is more lenient. To avoid chaos in the family, parents must present one mind to their children.

Live in the Present

Raising kids is a moment-to-moment affair. Each day demands on-the-spot decisions and judgments without benefit of all the facts. That is why happy parents live in the present. Looking back in guilt over a course of action that didn't turn out well drains our energies from the present. Looking fearfully ahead can create anxiety over what may come to pass but often doesn't.

You're Not Always Popular

All parents are disliked by their kids at times. This is a reality of healthy parenthood. Concerned parents base decisions on the long-term welfare of their children, but kids don't always understand that parents are acting in their best interests.

Teach Money Management

Many parents who house a leisure-loving college graduate complain, "My kid just doesn't understand the value of money." It is true that children who have never been accountable for their own money, never been forced to live within certain boundaries, and never had to do things for themselves will grow into dependent young adults who understand little about the value of money and the purpose of work. They can't—or won't—stand on their own two feet. As a result, when those same dependent young adults marry, not having been taught proper money management in their growing-up years, they soon receive a crash course in reality.

Money management is a part of our total life. The welfare of our marriages and families depends upon what we do with the money entrusted to us.

The divorce rate in America is climbing daily, and experts tell us that the lack of proper money management is one of the main contributing factors. Impulse spending, abuse of credit buying, and failure to consult the other partner in money matters, are just a few of the culprits wreaking havoc in the lives of young marrieds today.

It takes practice to understand how to use money wisely and responsibly. When we teach these lessons to our children, we instill in them the coping skills they need to succeed in life.

When we give our children clear, practical financial guidelines—by word and by example—we are much more likely to raise young adults ready to face this tough economic world, thereby giving them a precious gift: the key to self-sufficiency.

Nourish Love

Finally, for a Christian home to be successful, love must grow continuously and not be allowed to die. Love is the foundation of the family. Love leads two people into marriage; love also keeps them together. If children do not have the nourishment of love while they are small, they will develop a hard, rebellious attitude. There must be joy, gentleness, and love in the family to produce happy, normal children.

Love is sympathetic, is courteous, gives blessing for insult, avoids evil, pursues a peaceful lifestyle, does not keep score, never tries to get even, hardly notices when wronged, wishes the best for the loved one, is very patient and kind, and is never arrogant or self-seeking. (See I Corinthians 13.)

Responsible Living

Those seeking the applause of the world thumb their nose at responsible living. However, faithfulness or neglect in apparently small duties opens the door for life's blessings or its calamities. Little things are the test of character. Responsible living often includes doing undramatic and monotonous tasks of daily living.

The Bible teaches that we must provide the necessities of life for our families. If we fail in this basic duty we are "worse than an infidel"; to fail to provide for family needs is the same as to deny the faith (I Timothy 5:8).

People who are not willing to dutifully follow the path of responsible living have one major crisis after another. They often move from job to job, from one marriage to another, from one town to another. Apparently they are looking for the streets of gold on earth instead of the narrow path that leads to life—the path that is paved by self-forgetfulness, self-denial, and self-sacrifice.

If we are faithful in little things, God will call us to do greater things (Matthew 25:23; Luke 19:17). As we "hunger and thirst" for God's righteousness, He will fill us up! That yearning within is actually the voice of God calling us to a deeper walk with Him. When we yearn for God's will, that hunger and thirst will be satisfied.

It is not surprising that God calls people who are already busy with a task. He knows that the people who are carefully attending to the duties of life have learned to discipline themselves to use their time wisely. Moses was tending the sheep of his father-in-law when God spoke to him from the burning bush. While Zacharias was performing his usual Temple duty, God revealed His will about the birth of John the Baptist. David was dutifully watching sheep when he received the call to greater service. Matthew was working at his tax-collecting booth (his usual occupation) when Jesus called him to be a disciple. Peter, Andrew, James, and John were busy fishing and mending their nets (their usual duty) when Jesus called them to follow Him.

Few people realize the influence of these little things upon the development of character. God designs varied circumstances to test our faithfulness and to qualify us for greater trusts. Circumstances alone are not sufficient, but our reaction to circumstances tests our ability to stand true under pressure, to remain faithful to God regardless of what life brings.

Applause of God

To follow the path of responsible living, a person must be dependable and trustworthy on his secular job. He must be honest in his business dealings, controlling and managing his finances. He must discipline himself to say no to his desire for abundant possessions if they are detrimental to his spiritual walk with God. The path of responsible living calls him to happily say yes to the time-consuming years of rearing and molding his children to be not only faithful to God but also responsible citizens in society. It calls him to tenderly care for his aging parents, helping them to retain their self-respect and self-worth. It simply calls him to serve others in a spirit of self-forgetfulness. Jesus said that only as we lose our life for Him do we actually find it (Luke 9:24), and Jesus gave us His example to follow.

The applause of the world is not afforded to those who hunger and thirst for the things of God. By contrast, they are often ridiculed and mocked for living a quiet, undramatic, and seemingly humdrum life. They do not have great crowds cheering and following them, but more important than the applause of the world, they have the applause and the approval of God.

"Blessed are they which do hunger and thirst after righteousness: for they shall be filled."

Summary

True or False

1. In their music and lifestyle, some of today's superstars glamorize immorality by trampling underfoot the laws of God.

2. Following the trend of the world, in search of glamour and fantasy, mothers abandon toddlers; fathers desert their families.

3. Unwed mothers and absent fathers are the norm for children born into this group.

4. By contrast, a Christian home revolves around the moral as well as the spiritual teachings of Christ.

5. To succeed, a marriage must have commitment and oneness of purpose.

6. After marriage we should seek out the weaknesses of our partner and try to change them.

7. A strong marriage means insisting on your own viewpoint at all times.

8. In marriage, giving in at times to the likes and dislikes of the other is a weakness.

9. The success or failure of a marriage depends on appreciation and acknowledgment of each other's strengths and virtues, as well as on restraint from noticing each other's weaknesses and faults.

10. Responsible parenting means allowing a child to develop without discipline or a definite standard of conduct.

Answers

1. True, 2. True, 3. True, 4. True, 5. True, 6. False, 7. False, 8. False, 9. True, 10. False

6

Mercy or Judgment

The world's version:
"Blessed are those who judge: for they shall get even."

Jesus' version:
"Blessed are the merciful: for they shall obtain mercy."

Negative responses to situations of life result in failure to forgive, grumbling, complaining, and grudging. Keeping our feelings on our sleeve, we respond to circumstances of life by holding a grudge and feeling resentment.

Why do people nurture a grudge? Usually because they want pity and sympathy. They feel they have been done wrong and want to get even. Did Jesus hold a grudge? "Father, forgive them . . . " He prayed.

When a betrayed trust or fractured friendship stings us, we want to hold the grudge close, to nurse it, and to get even. But mercy and forgiveness refuse to be a party in paying the other person back. Instead, mercy chooses to hurt and to suffer—to accept undeserved suffering.

We suffer wrong, but instead of forgiving and forgetting, we find ourselves thinking the worst of the person who may or may not have injured us intentionally. Usually, if we allow ill feelings to fester in our heart, they have an embarrassing way of exposing themselves in word or deed. How a person reacts to mistreatment by others really indicates how much of Christ he has within his life.

We can't always change stressful situations, but we can defuse their impact on us by changing the way we handle them. The ability to forgive is one of the most important survival skills we can cultivate.

The world is full of people who establish their worth by degrading others. We should refuse to accept their insults. We must develop a thick skin. It is often easier to assume that people are doing the best they can and that many are simply unaware of the impact of their behavior.

It costs far more emotionally and mentally to defend ourselves constantly, to need to be right and in control. Let's try forgiving. Forgiveness will reduce tension, strengthen relationships, and increase joy. People who forgive are healthier and happier.

"But," we say, "if there is any justice in this universe, somebody must pay." That's true. The sinner may bear his own guilt—that's justice. Or the one sinned against may absorb what the sinner did—that's mercy. And that is what God did in Christ at Calvary. The holy nature of God demands justice for sin, and that justice was satisfied at Calvary. The sinless Lamb of God was offered up as an atonement for our sins. If God imparted mercy and forgiveness to us, shouldn't we do the same to our fellow man?

If we hold back forgiveness and mercy until the

offender deserves it, that's not forgiveness but justice. Here are some guidelines for true forgiveness:

1. We should forgive when we feel the first hurt.

2. There is no forgiveness without genuine acceptance of the other person as he is, not as we want him to be.

3. Forgiveness brings healing and reconciliation to fractured lives.

4. Forgiveness is not complete until the severed relationship is mended.

Mercy accepts not only the hurt received, it accepts the one who did the hurting, and it accepts the loss caused by the hurtful actions or words.

Only with the strength of Christ can we take definite steps to resist holding grudges:

1. Let God handle getting even.
2. Forgive at once.
3. Quietly endure the wrongs suffered.
4. Strive for peace with everyone.

Moods

Sometimes one face shows: a smile and sweet words. Then again, another face shows: angry words and a slammed door. And how quickly one can follow the other!

"It's just our moods," we say. Moods do change. Yes, we all have changing moods: frustration over daily problems, depression over circumstances gone wrong. But when daily frustrations and irritations erupt into anger on a regular basis, watch out! It's no longer a mood change of ordinary touchiness but an exploding situation of raw sensitivity and hurtful words when the least difficulty presents itself. For example:

1. Jealousy when someone else gets the promotion you wanted
2. Resentment when you goof and someone rubs it in
3. Insults you feel when someone criticizes you
4. Frustration when you just can't handle a situation

These are all situations when touchiness erupts into anger. The root cause of this type of anger springs from frustrations of the ego when a person's self-esteem is trampled upon. Such anger is a desire to punish others, to inflict suffering, to exact revenge for the hurt that we feel was inflicted on us.

This inner hostility is more than a mood change, yet it is a situation that the perfect love of the Savior can heal. If we will allow Him, He can direct us to discover His transforming, life-changing power. Through Him, there can be self-understanding, self-acceptance, and self-control.

Snobbery

Why is it easy to pass judgment on others? Sometimes it may be because of our own feelings of inferiority or superiority. We don't like to admit it, but we are all snobs in one way or another. There are certain types of individuals we are uncomfortable with, so we tend to avoid them altogether.

All snobbery has one thing in common: it is judgmental rather than merciful. A person can judge another person to be more or less important than himself because of:

1. Riches
2. Appearance
3. Talents
4. Education

What is your attitude when you are around the following people? Do you feel uncomfortable? Try to avoid them?

Someone who is:

1. Better looking than you
2. Richer than you
3. Poorer than you
4. Of a different religion
5. Of a different race
6. Handicapped
7. Talented
8. Important on his job and in his community
9. Smart and has good education
10. "Too nice"
11. Divorced
12. Widowed

Every person with whom we come in contact will not be our closest friend. However, we should be sensitive enough to the feelings of others not to be judgmental or snobbish. With the love of Christ in our hearts, we should learn how to make others feel important, needed, wanted, and loved.

Think of one person you are uncomfortable with and try to avoid. Or think of someone with whom you have difficulty showing your excitement about his or her successes. Or think of someone you have difficulty liking because he is different from you. Then, seek out that person and try to be an encourager in his life. In so doing, you will be blessed!

Apply Mercy

We should apply mercy to others in the way we would

want it applied to ourselves. True mercy is manifested in behavior.

1. We should offer praise and appreciation to others as we want to be appreciated.
2. We should listen to others as we want to be listened to.
3. We should pass on no gossip about another that we would not want circulated about us.
4. We should seek to understand others' viewpoints as we would want to be understood.
5. We should offer help to others where we would expect help.
6. We should give others the benefit of the doubt in questionable circumstances as we would want for ourselves.

Lessons from a Palomino

"Quick, come see who came to Sunday school," she exclaimed.

I had arrived at church early. Our ladies' group was in charge of cooking the Sunday dinner, and as I walked in the back door, this is how I was greeted.

As I turned the corner into the atrium area, my heart skipped a beat as I observed our Sunday morning visitor. There on the other side of the massive plate-glass windows, looking forlornly inside, was the most beautiful palomino horse I had ever seen. You could tell by the way he held his head and tossed his mane that he had good breeding, an aristocratic background.

"Oh, how beautiful!" I exclaimed as I walked closer to get a better view. Then I noticed that he was favoring one of his legs as if he might be hurt.

"He came to Sunday school; how nice!" someone else declared.

"What are we going to do?" was the question heard echoing from one to another.

"Maybe we had better call the police and see if they will come get him," we decided.

We phoned the local police station and were told that a palomino had been reported missing from a couple's home not far from our church. The dispatcher assured us that the owners would be contacted. Well, so much for our Sunday school visitor!

However, the owners were out looking for their escapee and could not be reached. What now?

While we were contemplating what to do next, one of the men of the church arrived. Not believing his own eyes, he walked to the front steps.

"Sure enough," we heard Brother Weaver say, "it is a horse." Finding a short rope, he draped it around the palomino's neck and attempted to lead him to a tree where he could be tied. As I watched, I noticed that the strong horse was limping but still desperately trying to disengage himself from the rope. Every inch an aristocrat, head held high, mane tossing, he was a picture to behold.

Excitement over, we returned to the kitchen to prepare fried chicken and all the trimmings.

"He escaped!" someone shouted, bursting into the kitchen.

"Where is he?" we wanted to know.

"Would you believe he went all the way around the building and is now looking forlornly into Pastor Spears's office?"

"Oh oh, we wouldn't let him come into Sunday school, so now he wants to talk to the pastor!" we joked.

Hastily wiping the flour off our hands, we went to look. There he was peering plaintively into our pastor's office. Now and then he took a bite of grass, trampling the flower beds as he favored his hurt leg.

The Sunday morning escapade ended shortly thereafter when the owners arrived. After being lavished with palomino kisses, they slipped on the halter and gently led our visitor away to home and safety.

I've been thinking about some of our people visitors who come to church. I have noticed their "good breeding" and "aristocratic" background. I have also noticed that some are "limping." Do they come having been drawn by the Spirit of God, and do we perhaps unconsciously attempt to put a rope around their neck by trying to make them conform to our wishes, being judgmental rather than extending mercy?

I noticed that the palomino gladly and willingly subjected himself to the owner's halter, lavishing his master with love. I have noticed also when visitors come, they too, in the process of time, willingly and gladly subject themselves to the Master. But do we give them time? Mercy instead of judgment?

We should treat every visitor with courtesy, respect, and dignity. Sometimes they are drawn to the church because they, as the palomino, are limping. When it is hard to walk, the going gets tough.

"Perhaps I can find comfort at the church," they may be saying. Do we give them comfort? Are we concerned that they are limping? Or are we too busy judging the reason for the limp? Sometimes the aristocrat has too much pride to admit that he is limping. He will hold up his head and go through all the motions when deep inside he hurts. But as with the palomino, once he recognizes the Master all is well.

Do we complain if our visitors attempt to find solace in the pastor's office? God forbid that we should be so selfish and snobbish. When they forlornly look to him for help, perhaps even trampling on the flower beds of his time, we should be in the background praying and holding them up before God. Help and comfort should be available to all who seek it. Our responsibility is not to judge but to extend mercy, to love and to care for them as God draws them into His family.

Lessons from a Sinner Man

A certain man went down from Dallas to Longview. "Maybe I can find a job in Longview," he reasoned.

Unemployment had dogged his footsteps and been his constant companion for months now as he pounded the streets of Dallas in vain. Someone had told him that Longview was "flowing with milk and honey."

As he began to make the rounds of the employment agencies, the young man realized he had made a mistake. The flowing milk and honey turned out to be, in reality, a dried-up oil industry that had shut down the resources of this once-thriving East Texas city.

Weeks passed. The young man, going from employer to employer, soon exhausted his meager supply of funds.

Out of money and out of a job, this certain young man fell among the thieves of despair, which stripped him of his dignity, robbed him of his self-respect, wounded him with fears of destitution, and then departed, leaving him half dead.

By chance, a certain preacher (Reverend Pree Occupyde) crossed the young man's path. Preoccupied with thoughts on his upcoming sermon text on "the good Samaritan," the preacher scarcely noticed the young man. The vacant, staring eyes and the slump of dejected shoulders went unnoticed as the preacher, mulling over in his head his three sermon points on the priest, the Levite, and the Samaritan, passed him by.

Likewise, a certain member of the church (Brother Seth Rychus), returning from the men's weekly prayer meeting at the church, happened by the certain young man. Noticing what the thieves of despair had done to him by robbing him of a job and his self-respect and human dignity, the church member approached the young man. Feeling as though he had discharged his religious duty, the self-righteous church member said, "Bless you, brother," then departed on the other side.

But a certain sinner man (Mr. Ben There), with no religious background or religious affiliation at all, happened upon the destitute young man and had compassion on him, thinking to himself, I know how the young man feels; I've been there!

The sinner man bound up the young man's wounded spirit, pouring in the oil of friendship and human compassion. He listened with concern as the young man told him how the thieves of despair had robbed him of his faith in humankind; how he had been stripped of all dignity and self-respect and now had no money and no one to turn to.

Finally, the sinner man put the young man in his car and drove him to the Holiday Inn. The sinner man then fed the destitute young man, paid his hotel bill, and told the surprised innkeeper that whatever other charges the young man incurred while he was searching for a job he would come again and repay.

When the sinner man left the young man thought, "If a sinner man, whom the church considers an outcast, will rescue a destitute man in trouble, what a reflection it is on the church members and their religion if, in indifference, they pass the needy by."

The Mysterious Stranger

Tears streamed down his face but he refused to retaliate. He was talked about unjustly, yet the eyes were kind behind the tears.

I wonder who he is?

Life is complex, hurried, and self-centered in this modern day we live in. Yet, amid all of life's complexities, every once in a while he emerges—this mysterious stranger.

What is his name?

I saw him the other day in the eyes of a father. The teenage boy had rejected the father's teachings, turned his back and walked away, yet, there in the midst of rebellion, was the mysterious stranger.

I recognized him one day in the actions of a destitute mother as she neglected her own self to provide for her child. Ignoring the pangs of hunger in her own body, she cheerfully and willingly provided food for her young.

I saw him in the home. There was no quarreling or bitterness, because he was there. The family was content, because he was there.

He is tender-hearted, gentle, the only reason for

being. He makes life rich and worthwhile—this mysterious stranger.

He emerges from the pages of the Bible as I read about the Man from Galilee. I see him once again as Jesus ascends the cross and allows Himself to be nailed there. As I read about the life, death, and resurrection of the Savior, I see the mysterious stranger standing in the shadows radiating the magnetism that makes me ask again, Who is he? What is his name?

I see him in all the good things of life.

He is longsuffering, kind, does not envy, is never pushy.

He does not behave himself unseemly, seeks not his own comfort, is not easily provoked, thinks evil of no one.

He rejoices not in iniquity but rejoices in the truth.

He bears all things (never retaliates), believes all things (never doubts), hopes all things (even under the most adverse circumstances), endures all things (years of self-denial without complaint). (See I Corinthians 13:4-7.)

I wonder who he is—this mysterious stranger.

What is his name?

Don't you know?

Haven't you recognized him?

His name is simply Love and Mercy.

"Blessed are the merciful: for they shall obtain mercy."

Summary

True or False

1. Usually, people nurture grudges because they want pity and sympathy.

2. The ability to forgive is one of the most important survival skills we can cultivate.

3. One of the definitions of mercy is retaliation.

4. Mercy means holding back forgiveness until the offender deserves it.

5. When daily frustrations erupt into anger on a regular basis, the problem ceases to be only a mood change of ordinary touchiness but becomes an exploding situation.

6. Avoiding those who are of a different race, different religion, or those who are good looking, talented, smart, nice, important, rich, or poor, is called snobbery.

7. True mercy is manifested in behavior. The sinner man (Mr. Ben There) bound up the young man's wounded spirit, pouring in the oil of friendship and human compassion.

8. Love and Mercy bears all things (never retaliates) believes all things (never doubts), hopes all things (even under the most adverse circumstances), endures all things (without complaint).

9. Love and Mercy ignores the viewpoint of others, refuses to offer praise and appreciation to others, is jealous of others' good fortune.

10. Love and Mercy is quick to judge, quick to jump to conclusions, and quick to exact revenge.

Answers

1. True, 2. True, 3. False, 4. False, 5. True, 6. True, 7. True, 8. True, 9. False, 10. False

7

Gossipers or Pure in Heart

The world's version:
"Blessed are the gossipers: for they shall be rewarded by seeing reputations destroyed."

Jesus' version:
"Blessed are the pure in heart: for they shall see God."

"Plain ole gossip" (repeating something scandalous that one has heard, whether true or not) has wrecked more lives possibly than drugs or alcohol. Gossip scars the inner person.

There was a man once—a good man, a God-fearing man, a church man. He had some laying hens, and daily he gathered the eggs and delivered them to his regular customers. One day a fellow church member saw him coming out of a liquor store, egg basket in hand. The church member could not wait to pass along this new tidbit of information. Consequently, the story ran rampant through the church, "Brother So-and-So was seen coming out of a liquor store."

Then (as repeated gossip does) the story was expanded and embellished. "Brother So-and-So was seen coming out of a liquor store—he was drunk, staggering, couldn't walk" and so on.

What people didn't know was that Brother So-and-So went into the liquor store to deliver his eggs to a regular customer, the owner. His heart was pure and so he assumed others' hearts were too. Because of vicious gossip, Brother So-and-So's reputation and inner man were scarred. He quit delivering eggs to the liquor store owner for fear of more gossip. That man was my father-in-law.

Respect

No one likes to be put down, laughed at, made fun of, or gossiped about. We are all offended by the rude acts of others toward us. We should be thoughtful of others and careful not to harass, annoy agitate, antagonize, or provoke. Proper behavior is of the utmost importance.

Proper behavior starts in the home. Parents need to teach their children to have respect for others. Let us remember that we teach our kids more by our conduct than by our words. As I grew up, my dad was a man of very few words, but he taught me by example—by the way he lived and by the person he was. He taught me to respect him because he showed respect for me.

If we teach respect for one another in the confines of our homes, it will not be difficult to apply it to the remaining areas of our lives.

Words Cut Deep

"The words of a talebearer are as wounds, and they go down into the innermost parts of the belly" (Proverbs 18:8). Words can cut deep. Some people delight in carrying tales.

"Pleasant words are as an honeycomb, sweet to the soul, and health to the bones" (Proverbs 16:24). Man is both spirit and body. Kind words minister to the total person in a positive way. A crushed spirit can make us physically ill, but kind words are a healing balm to both body and spirit.

Be a healer, not a hurter. Use pleasant words. Using pleasant words to encourage others is a skill every one of us can develop. In fact, it usually doesn't come naturally. It takes practice.

Pleasant words spoken with a false motive are flattery. By contrast, words that heal are words spoken in the proper way and are primarily for the benefit of the hearer—not for the one who has uttered the words. A sincere, kind word can cheer us up!

Do you have a Christ-controlled tongue?

1. Can you be trusted one hundred percent with a confidence? Can you keep a secret?

2. Can you speak compliments and kind words?

3. Have you ever pointed out some good point about a person when everyone else in the group was tearing him apart?

4. When recognition and praise is given to another, are you offended? Do you say spiteful things?

5. Do you shun the very appearance of gossip? If your friend is doubted by others, can you speak up in his behalf?

Benjamin Franklin said, "I will speak ill of no man, and speak all the good I know of everybody."

Our ability to communicate through speech is one of God's greatest gifts to man. But like so many other things that are a part of our life, we can easily misuse this great gift of speech. Gossip is a misuse of God's gift.

"But the tongue no man can tame," (James 3:8). It is a battle we will always have to fight, but with a Christ-controlled heart there can be a Christ-controlled tongue.

"Set a watch, O LORD, before my mouth; keep the door of my lips" (Psalm 141:3).

The Conscious and Subconscious Mind

Jesus said, "Out of the abundance of the heart the mouth speaketh" (Matthew 12:34). Sooner or later we discover what type of person we are talking with. As one person communicates with another, whatever he has fed into his mind will come forth in his speech. To control our tendency to gossip, we must control what we feed our minds. What goes into our minds eventually comes out in our speech.

Psychology has loosely divided our mind into what we call our conscious mind and our subconscious mind. Our conscious mind is the part of our mind with which we knowingly think. It is the part of our mind with which we form habits, make decisions, make judgments, and reason. It is the part of our mind over which we have control.

We only have an influence over our subconscious mind, but over our conscious mind we have control. We do not always make use of this gift from God, this ability to control our thoughts, but we do have it. With our conscious mind the choice of what we do is completely ours.

Everything we hear, see, read, think about, or act upon goes first into our conscious mind and then is deposited into our subconscious. We can control our conscious mind by discipline and bring some manner of order to it. But if we do not control what drops into our subconscious, we have no active means of controlling it.

When I was learning to type, my fingers at first felt awkward on the keys. I had too many thumbs or not enough fingers. But as time progressed and I practiced my exercises and finger positions, gradually I became proficient and skillful in the use of the typewriter. Why?

At first, I was conscious of every key and of the movement of every finger. But as I practiced and fed into my conscious mind the necessary data, that data was transferred from the conscious to the subconscious, and from the subconscious comes proficiency and skill. If I tried to be painstakingly careful and conscious of every finger movement, invariably errors occurred. But through practice, correct thought patterns were transferred from the conscious to the subconscious, and it wasn't long until I became proficient and accurate. The secret lay in depositing in the mind the correct finger locations and exercises. Whatever was deposited in the conscious mind, whether correct or incorrect, is what came forth from the subconscious.

The person we eventually become depends upon what we feed our minds. "Whatsoever a man soweth, that shall he also reap" (Galatians 6:7). We cannot sow something evil and reap something pure. The law of the harvest will not allow it.

Day by day we are molding our character, and what we feed our minds comes forth in our speech. Out of the subconscious comes the real you. Envy, jealousy, and malice fed to the mind come forth in gossip, backbiting, and general ill-will.

Sometimes young people cannot understand why we teach and preach against certain kinds of music. They do not understand that as the beat and words constantly bombard the conscious mind, gradually the filth is transferred to the subconscious and becomes a part of their personality and the looseness of this world will sooner or later manifest itself in their lives.

Often, successful businessmen will not make a major decision until they sleep on it. They know that if they have fed their mind with honest business practices and concepts, somewhere in their subconscious these facts and wisdom lurk. The subconscious never sleeps, so while the businessman is relaxed and asleep his subconscious sifts facts, organizes and compares them, and then brings to his conscious mind the right decision to make.

How many times have you or I been in this very situation? We agonize over a decision we must make. We worry, fret, cry, and feel at a loss. Then one morning we get up and out of the blue we know the answer. Our subconscious sifts through all the facts it has been fed, compares those facts, selects the most appropriate from the facts it has, and then comes forth with the answer we need to know.

In making a decision the mind:

1. Identifies the problem
2. Determines the alternatives by facts it knows
3. Compares the alternatives
4. Selects the most appropriate

The secret of a wise decision or unwise one lies in the facts we feed our mind. The mind works on whatever we feed it, whether correct or incorrect, good or evil.

Our mind grows on what we feed it. The more we read and study the Bible, feeding our mind with Scripture, the more our subconscious will take over and bring to memory good thoughts, good and pure ideas. God speaks to us in various ways, and one of the ways is through our mind. If we have fed our mind on the pure Word of God, then God can reach deep into our subconscious and bring a passage of Scripture to memory that we have read. It may provide the answer we are seeking to some problem. Our conscious mind may have forgotten the passage of Scripture, but the subconscious did not. God will use our subconscious for His glory if we feed it His Word.

On the other hand, if we feed our mind on the trash of this world, our subconscious will only bring forth trash, filth, and evil. The law of the harvest prevails.

Our subconscious is a valuable asset if we will learn how to feed it properly.

Pure in Heart

Jesus said, "Blessed are the pure in heart." Who are the pure in heart? II Corinthians 5:17 tells us, "Therefore if any man be in Christ, he is a new creature." God is more concerned about our truly being a new creation than anything else. He knows that if we are right in our inward being, we will certainly do right in our outward actions. The essential thing is character (being).

Holiness, or purity, is an attribute of the nature of God. The word in Hebrew and also in Greek simply means separation. God is separated from sin. Sin cannot stand in the presence of God, for God is holy, separate from sin. As sinners, we must be clothed with the righteousness of Christ, purchased by His atoning death.

When we are born again we receive God's nature in our hearts. Since holiness, or purity, is an attribute of the nature of God, through the new-birth experience we receive a holy, pure nature, a nature that separates us from sin. The Holy Spirit of God comes to take up residence in our hearts.

The new nature does not replace our old nature but dwells alongside our carnal human nature to subdue it. Although the Spirit of God in our hearts hates sin and shrinks from it, our Adamic nature with its sinful tendencies is still very much alive and is attracted by the allure of the world.

A new convert may not understand this concept. He experiences the thrill of being forgiven and the joy of being born into the family of God, but then something happens. His sinful nature rears its ugly head. It was not eradicated in the new-birth process as he may have thought, but it is very much alive!

Temptations and worldly desires still plague him. At this point, he may give up his Christian walk and go back to a life of sin because he becomes confused when old temptations and old tendencies assail him. In doing so, he expresses a misconception of the Christian life, falsely assuming that all will be bliss now that Jesus lives in his heart. The problem is simply that his Adamic nature is trying once again to gain control.

Being tempted is not sin. The Bible teaches that Jesus was tempted in all points as we are, yet without sin (Hebrews 4:15). Only when we yield to temptations do we sin.

The Spirit of God lives in our hearts and desires to rule our thoughts and actions. When we yield to God's control, His holy attributes are manifested in our lives. The holiness (purity) of God is then visible for all to see through our attitudes and manner of life.

But when we suppress God and allow our own human

nature to have mastery in our lives, then come forth carnal desires, old habits, and sinful tendencies (such as gossip). God does not control us like robots: He allows us to choose which nature will have mastery in our lives.

As we walk with the Lord and learn to yield to Him day by day, the old, sinful desires become less powerful. As we yield to God's holy and pure nature, we develop a hunger to be more like Him.

When we allow God to control our thought processes and our actions, then the transforming power of God is apparent for all to see. As Jesus lives in us, we become transparent and His holy attributes shine forth. The controlling inward nature will manifest itself outwardly. As a result, our outward conduct, which the world beholds, will correspond to the inner urgings of the Spirit of God.

If we elevate God to His rightful place in our lives, His transforming power will mold us, change us, and impute to us His holy nature, making us the "pure in heart."

"Blessed are the pure in heart: for they shall see God."

Summary

True or False

1. Gossip is okay if you only repeat what is true.
2. Kind words are a healing balm to both body and spirit.
3. What we feed our minds comes forth in our speech.
4. Envy, jealousy, and malice fed to the mind come forth in gossip, backbiting, and general ill-will.
5. Our subconscious mind will reject any unpure thoughts and will only store up what is good.
6. If we feed our mind on the trash of this world, our subconscious will bring forth good and pure thoughts and ideas.
7. Our subconscious mind is a valuable asset if we will learn how to feed it properly.
8. When we allow God to control our thought processes and our actions, then the transforming power of God is apparent for all to see.
9. It doesn't matter how we act toward others as long as we have a pure heart.
10. If we are right in our inward being, we will certainly do right in our outward actions.

Answers

1. False, 2. True, 3. True, 4. True, 5. False, 6. False, 7. True, 8. True, 9. False, 10. True

8

Agitators or Peacemakers

The world's version:
"Blessed are the agitators: for they will transfer their discontentment to others."

Jesus' version:
"Blessed are the peacemakers: for they shall be called the children of God."

It's not hard to recognize the agitators of this world. They are the ones continually grumbling, grudging, griping, and whining. Their discontentment is rooted in selfishness. They are caught up in possession expectations. There's always another "thing" they don't have, another "pleasure" they haven't experienced, and they will trample the feelings of others to gain these things.

The increase of things creates an appetite for more. However, more is never enough; thus the agitation of discontent and restlessness is transferred to others by the continual clawing and scratching for more.

Trying to keep up with the Joneses has always been our downfall. The Joneses get a new car; we must have a new car. The Joneses get a bigger house; we must have a bigger house. And on and on it goes. Not being content and continually reaching for more wreaks havoc in homes today. Discontentment turns to agitation. For example:

"Why can't you make more money?"

"I want a new dress. Sue's husband bought her one last week."

"I want new furniture. Martha has a new couch."

"I want this. So-and-So has one."

"I want that—"

"I want—"

"I want—"

The divorce rate in America is climbing, and experts tell us that the lack of proper money management is the biggest culprit. The root cause of a lack of proper money management lies in buying things we can't afford. And we buy them simply to keep up with others. We have become enslaved by expectations that cannot be satisfied. The more we have, the more we want.

Solomon was the wealthiest of men, yet he found that the accumulation of things and the pursuit of pleasure did not bring lasting happiness. In the Book of Ecclesiastes, Solomon revealed from personal experience that all earthly goals, when pursued as ends in themselves, lead to dissatisfaction, discontent, and restlessness. If one tries to find satisfaction and fulfillment in the fleeting pleasures of life, he is doomed to failure. Life on this plane is empty and meaningless.

Pursuit of Pleasure

Have you ever ridden an exciting roller coaster? After the thrilling ride, what did you want to do? You wanted to find a more exciting ride. Why? Because the pleasure is temporary. It does not really satisfy. The thrill just gives a craving for more.

Everyone likes comedians. They make us laugh. The more jokes they tell, the more we want them to tell. It's always, "Tell me a funnier story; I'm still not satisfied."

By chasing after pleasure, humanity seeks to make life simply fun and games, thereby winking at sin and embracing it.

"Wine is a mocker, strong drink is raging: and whosoever is deceived thereby is not wise" (Proverbs 20:1). Truly, many in our world today are deceived by strong drink. Alcoholism is on the rise, yet an alcoholic knows that alcohol does not satisfy. Why does one then become an alcoholic? A person becomes an alcoholic by taking just one drink. When that first drink does not totally satisfy, then he is deceived into thinking that more will do the trick. He drinks more and more until he becomes addicted and cannot quit. The more he drinks, the more he craves.

The same is true of drug addiction. The initial high brings a craving for more and more. It's a vicious cycle, a merry-go-round. In alcoholism and drug addiction, people are seeking something to satisfy. Instead of turning to God, who is the only satisfier, they seek happiness by chasing after the elusive pleasures of this world. Nightclubs and bars are crammed with men and women searching frantically for something to satisfy. Entertainment and fleeting pleasures are only temporal and will not bring lasting peace.

People in every generation look for happiness in the wrong place—in physical gratification and in the possession of material things. Life is a cycle. A new generation comes and the old one passes away, but the new generation does not learn from the old. History repeats itself.

The roots of restlessness and discontent are thus fiercely connected to our reaching for more. Discontent drives us to a life of hurt and pressure. By transferring our discontent to others, we become agitators.

Peacemakers

Jesus said, "Blessed are the peacemakers" (not the agitators). Who are the peacemakers of this world? Obviously, the agitators are the ones who seek to gratify self. Selfishness separates, but love binds together. Love is God's adhesive power. Selfishness seeks its own, but love "Vaunteth not itself . . . seeketh not her own" (I Corinthians 13:4-5). Selfishness contracts to include only self, but true love expands to include others.

An agitator is self-centered, self-willed, and selfish. On the other hand, a peacemaker is one who has developed a strong sensitivity to the feelings of other people, one who likes harmony, one who can persuade, conciliate, and help others appreciate themselves, one who is truly unselfish.

Some people may be peace-loving but are not peacemakers. They do not do anything about creating peace. The peacemaker goes about his business quietly sowing his seed, confident that someday there will be a harvest of righteousness.

The peacemaker leads others to the riches of Christ, not by compromise and tolerance, but by creating an open door of reconciliation to the sinner. Jesus, who is the Prince of Peace, refused to surrender to unrighteousness by compromise. Instead, He attacked, sin, but not the sinner.

Being a peacemaker requires tact, wisdom, courage, and love. The agitator is irritable, conceited, and selfish, whereas the peacemaker is conciliatory, tactful, and courageous, ready to do all he or she can do to make peace. This can only be accomplished in the same manner that Jesus did it—by personal sacrifice.

Sometimes a peacemaker is called upon to be a "living sacrifice."

Living Sacrifice

"Present your bodies a living sacrifice" (Romans 12:1). "Living sacrifice" is an oxymoron, a figure of speech in which words of opposite meaning or suggestion are used together. "Living" and "sacrifice" are words of opposite meaning. When we sacrifice something, it dies. What then is a "living sacrifice"? The rest of the verse says, "holy, acceptable unto God, which is your reasonable service." My life is to be acceptable to God by being a living sacrifice.

One interesting dictionary definition of the word "sacrifice" is this: "In baseball, a bunt allowing a base runner to advance while the batter is put out; also, a fly ball allowing a runner to score after the catch." In other words, the batter pulls back his own performance and "sacrifices" for the runner. This is teamwork. Allowing the runner to advance for the ultimate good of the team, the batter becomes a living sacrifice.

It's not fun being a sacrifice. For example, parents sacrifice time and money for the correct upbringing of their children. They place their children's needs above their own dreams and desires.

I am sure that in the game of baseball the batter

would like to hit the ball with all his strength, but the coach says, "It's time for the sacrifice play for the ultimate good of the team."

In the spiritual realm, God expects us to live in a manner that will lead others to Him, sacrificing our time and energy. In other words, our life becomes the bunt that allows a base runner to advance while the batter is put out and also the fly ball allowing a runner to score after the catch. Our Coach is calling the plays if we will but follow.

The Honey-Pot Ant

Ants live and work together with other ants in groups called colonies. They cannot survive alone. Each worker ant has its own job to perform. Inside the anthill, or nest, each ant basically goes about its particular duty. Without an overseer, the ant does what needs to be done when it should be done. It anticipates future needs and prepares for them well in advance.

Some ants feed and care for the young. Others keep the nest clean. Others store the food. Others collect food and bring it into the storehouse. Others make the nest bigger. Still others guard the entrances to the nest. They defend the nest against enemies that will creep in. They are all working together for one purpose: self-preservation.

God placed within all His creatures (whether it be insect, animal, or human) the instinct of self-preservation. Instinctively, the ants know as they go about storing up food in their nests that a day is coming when they cannot gather and collect food. In wintertime they rest underground in their nests while in summertime they busily prepare for the winter day they know is coming. By instinct, they know to keep their storehouse full, just as we should know by instinct to keep our spiritual storehouse full. Jesus Himself said, "The night cometh, when no man can work" (John 9:4).

Ants work together in unity and harmony, reaching toward a common goal, but sometimes we, as the children of God, bicker and strive with one another. Forgetting our common goal, we concentrate on individual passions, letting jealousy, envy and bitterness hinder God's work in our midst. Ants realize they cannot survive alone, but we tend to forget that we need others.

One species of ants is called the honey ant. Honey ants live on sweet juices that they collect from flowers and green plants. These ants do not eat anything else and will die if there are no green plants.

To prepare for times when they cannot find any green plants, honey ants will store the sweet juices in their nest. They do not make cups of wax or paper to store the juice as bees or wasps do. Instead, they use their own body to store up the honey.

A few young ants will keep swallowing honey until they become round as peas. They become too fat to walk or to work. These are called "honey-pot ants." Then they will suspend themselves from the ceiling of the nest. For the rest of their lives they hang by their feet from the ceiling. When hungry ants come for food, these storage ants give up honey through their mouths. They have dedicated and consecrated their very lives for a purpose: that others might live.

This is a graphic illustration of Paul's words, "present your bodies a living sacrifice." God does not ask us literally to sacrifice our body as the honey-pot ant does, but He expects us to live our life in such a manner as to reveal Him to a lost and dying world, sacrificing time and energy for others.

The peacemakers of this world do not portray the selfishness of the agitators who say, "Gimme, gimme more." Instead, they portray sacrificial living for others.

"Blessed are the peacemakers: for they shall be called the children of God."

Summary

True or False

1. The accumulation of things and the pursuit of pleasure will bring lasting happiness.
2. The roots of restlessness and discontent are fiercely connected to our reaching for more.
3. The increase of things creates an appetite for more.
4. Solomon found satisfaction and fulfillment in the fleeting pleasures of life.
5. By transferring our discontent to others we become agitators.
6. A peacemaker, in order to create peace, must compromise.
7. A peacemaker is one who has developed a strong sensitivity to the feelings of other people, who likes harmony, and who can persuade, conciliate, and help others appreciate themselves.
8. A "living sacrifice" is someone who gripes when he has to spend time and energy with others.
9. In the game of baseball, a bunt allowing a base runner to advance while the batter is put out is called a sacrifice play. Allowing the runner to advance for the ultimate good of the team, the batter becomes a "living sacrifice."
10. The honey-pot ant has dedicated and consecrated its very life for a purpose: that others might live.

Answers

1. False, 2. True, 3. True, 4. False, 5. True, 6. False, 7. True, 8. False, 9. True, 10. True

9

Standing Up or Blending In

The world's version:
"Blessed are those who conform to the crowd: for they will blend in."

Jesus' version:
"Blessed are they which are persecuted for righteousness' sake: for theirs is the kingdom of heaven."

We cannot help others to learn lessons that we ourselves have not learned before God. The more thorough our training, the greater will be our usefulness in God's work. A proud person cannot deal with someone else who has the same condition. A hypocrite cannot touch the hypocrisy in another, nor can one who is loose in his life have a helpful effect on one who suffers the same difficulty. If such is our nature, we will not be able to condemn it in others; we, in fact, can hardly recognize it in others. We will conform to the crowd and blend in.

A doctor may cure others without curing himself, but this is not true in the spiritual realm. What we have not seen we cannot show others. Where we have not trodden we cannot lead others. What we have not learned we cannot teach others. The elusive quality of the spirit expresses itself in a person's nature.

For example, someone may mentally condemn pride, jealousy, or hypocrisy yet not sense these things in his own spirit. Thus, when these things appear in another, his spirit is not distressed; in fact, it may even be sympathetic. Then the day comes when God's Spirit so works in his life that he sees what pride, or jealousy, or hypocrisy is really like. Now every time one of these spirits appear in another, he senses its ugliness and is distressed.

What he has learned and seen from God enables him to sense and to be distressed. Now that he recognizes this ailment in his own life, he can help someone else. This is how we come to spiritual knowledge. Spiritual sensitivity comes about only through many dealings—God's Spirit touching our spirit and we, in turn, touching someone else—not through conforming to the world's standards but standing up for God.

The "In Crowd"

Many people work hard to be accepted by a particular group. To be in the "in crowd" usually means that everything else must be put in second place. People often relegate personal beliefs, self-respect, and responsibilities to second place in order to stay "in." Social pressure is hard to resist.

What makes people susceptible to group pressure? People need:

1. Acceptance
2. Security
3. Identity

Being accepted by someone we consider important is a way of reassuring ourselves that we are okay. The need to be accepted sometimes makes us compromise our principles to conform to the group.

Relying on the security that comes from being accepted by the "in crowd" delays the hard job of developing an inner security that is not dependent on others.

Young people think that belonging to a particular group furnishes them an identity. Everyone knows who they are because of special clothes and similar hair styles. This type of identity is dependent on conformity to the crowd.

Belonging to an exclusive group, the "in crowd," can help meet the basic needs of acceptance, security, and identity. However, the end result of conformity is that individuality is suppressed; therefore, beliefs may be compromised, feelings ignored, and lives endangered by going too far with the crowd.

The apostle Paul warned God's people not to chase after the approval of other people but instead to look for God's approval (Galatians 1:10). Paul stressed independence and emphasized that we should learn personal responsibility (Galatians 6:4-5).

God intends for our lives to be like a piece of clay. Clay can be molded and changed by the potter, but it remains unchanged by its environment. Put a piece of clay in a jar and it stays the same. It does not conform to the container like water. It has a form of its own, but it is pliable to the Master's touch. We should have a mind that is open to the voice of God but closed to the call of the world, unchanged by our environment. We must stand up for God rather than blend in with the world.

Doubt or Faith

Doubt runs rampant in the lives of those who blend in with the world. Faith gives us the backbone to stand up for God and personal convictions, but doubt dissolves that backbone and makes a wishy-washy individual. He wavers and is blown about by the gust of unbelief and doubt, thereby blending in with whatever comes his way.

What is faith? Many times we try to make something very complicated out of faith, but faith is simply believing what God says. It is an assurance and conviction that God's Word is true.

Hebrews 11:1 says, "Now faith is the substance of things hoped for, the evidence of things not seen." The Amplified Bible's version of the same verse is this: "Now faith is the assurance (the confirmation, the title-deed) of the things (we) hope for, being the proof of things (we) do not see and the conviction of reality—faith perceiving as real fact what is not revealed to the sense."

When God says something in His Word, faith is simply believing that it is so, whether or not there is any evidence to support the statement. God honors our faith and will bring to pass in our lives what He has promised, if we will simply believe.

Faith defies reason. It does not always face visible facts, but it perceives as "real fact" what the sense cannot discern. Faith never gives up; it is always victorious.

Evading Responsibility

Mrs. Pilate was napping. Her husband was up and about his official business of governing; the day was proceeding. Suddenly, Mrs. Pilate's nap was interrupted by a very disturbing dream concerning that fellow from Nazareth.

As the day wore on this man Jesus was brought before Pilate. Disturbed, Mrs. Pilate begged her husband to have nothing to do with this just man, "for I have suffered many things this day in a dream because of him" (Matthew 27:19). He disregarded her dream and her pleadings. Pilate succumbed to the cry of the crowd to "crucify him!"

If Pilate had listened to his heart ("I find no fault in him") and stood up for his personal convictions instead of yielding to the pressures of the crowd, he would not have handed Jesus over to be crucified. In our world today there are some who (like Pilate) have compromised their own inner convictions and have been swayed by the pressures of the crowd to "crucify him."

Pilate failed the first requirement in being a leader. A leader must have the ability to lead regardless of controversy. He must be strong in personal convictions, not afraid to take a stand for moral values and ethical decisions regardless of outside pressures.

Strong leaders are the ones who take the forefront. They are the first to choose a direction, a plan. They have the courage to act on inner convictions, taking responsibility for those actions regardless of influential persons. Noneffective leaders concentrate on the difficulties rather than the possibilities and usually compromise their convictions by conforming to outside pressure. Pilate became known as the ruler who conformed to the cry of the crowd by evading responsibility in the trial of Christ.

Guidelines and Boundaries

Ethical decision-making is not an automatic response. Rather, it seems to be an ongoing process that develops day by day. The guidelines and boundaries we abide by daily contribute to the development of ethical and moral decision-making. These guidelines and boundaries will help a person to stand up for convictions rather than conform to the pressures of the crowd.

Some parents today discipline their children with a weak, "That really isn't very becoming behavior," instead of instituting guidelines and boundaries. Having definite boundaries makes a person feel secure and protected rather than restricted. Insecure adults are those who were denied boundaries as children. Decision-making is difficult for them, because without guidelines and boundaries there can be no strong inner convictions as to what moral concepts are all about.

Contrary to popular belief, guidelines do not squelch creative powers but rather enhance them, giving the freedom to be creative. Knowing he must suffer consequences if he violates boundaries gives a person the incentive needed to develop within those boundaries.

Personal values are instilled in a child at an early age. Parents, church, and school all play their part in the values a child ultimately chooses. The development of these personal values determines whether or not in later life an individual will stand up for personal convictions or blend in with the crowd.

The Courage of Our Convictions

Jesus said that we would be persecuted for righteousness' sake (Matthew 5:10). What did He mean? He meant we should have the courage of our convictions, the courage to stand alone if necessary.

Pilate did not display the courage of his own convictions but was swayed by the crowd. When others conform to the crowd and blend in with the world, God's people should have the courage to make choices, not because "others are doing it" or "will I be accepted if I do it?" but because "it is right." If we choose to live this way, Jesus said we would be persecuted, but He also said we would be blessed (happy).

The prophet Jeremiah was a most unlikely man for the task to which God called him. He was by nature a tender-hearted and somewhat timid person, but God called him to proclaim an unpopular message. Jeremiah faced pressures to compromise his message and conform to the attitude prevalent in his day, but through it all he was a faithful servant of the Lord. Despite imprisonment and threats of death, Jeremiah refused to deny his personal convictions in order to be accepted by the group. He had to stand alone and declare God's message, though it was unpopular, to an unbelieving generation.

There will also come a time in our lives when we will have to stand alone. We will face peer pressure to deny our personal convictions in order to be accepted by the group. God's children must be prepared to stand alone.

If we do things "because they are right" we will have a serene and peaceful spirit. We will not constantly think, What did I say to this one, to that one? What did I do yesterday, today? Righteous living brings calmness to the doer.

On the other hand, it brings conviction to the onlooker, which, in turn, evokes antagonism. Therefore, we can expect to be persecuted for right living.

One day a great crowd of people mocked the first Christians. "These men are full of new wine," they said

(Acts 2:13). These Christians had experienced Pentecost, but while some of them were fretting about what to do, Peter stood up and began to speak. He didn't stop to think whether or not he had the ability to speak in public or whether he had a sermon to give. He began to share what he felt overflowing his heart, and that day three thousand people were converted (Acts 2:41).

Since those first Christians were already being mocked, a person who wished to blend in would have thought about the consequences of being ridiculed still further and would have kept silent. An opportunity to change his world would have been lost. But some people are not afraid to make mistakes; some are not afraid to fail. Some, like Peter, have the courage to dare, the courage to dream and to fail, the courage to pick themselves up and to dream again. They refuse to conform to the crowd by blending in, but choose instead to stand up for Jesus.

"Blessed are they which are persecuted for righteousness' sake: for theirs is the kingdom of heaven."

Summary

True or False

1. People are susceptible to group pressure because they need acceptance, security, and identity and feel a particular group can help meet these needs.

2. The need to be accepted sometimes makes us compromise our principles to conform to the group.

3. The end result of conformity to the crowd is that individuality is suppressed; therefore, beliefs may be compromised, feelings ignored, and lives endangered by going too far with the crowd.

4. Relying on the security that comes from being accepted by the "in crowd" delays that hard job of developing an inner security that is not dependent on others.

5. Boundaries and guidelines squelch creativity.

6. Having definite boundaries makes a person feel secure and protected rather than restricted.

7. In the trial of Jesus, Pilate stood up for his own personal convictions rather than succumbing to the pressures of the crowd.

8. Faith is too complicated to understand; therefore, God will honor our doubt.

9. Jeremiah was a prophet who compromised his message when faced with outside pressures and conformed to the unbelieving attitude prevalent in his day.

10. When others conform to the crowd and blend in with the world, God's people should have the courage to stand up for their convictions, the courage to stand alone if necessary.

Answers

1. True, 2. True, 3. True, 4. True, 5. False, 6. True, 7. False, 8. False, 9. False, 10. True

10

Shallow Faith or Committed Disciple

The world's version:
"Blessed are those who have shallow faith: for when they are accused of being a Christian there will not be enough evidence to convict them."

Jesus' version:
"Blessed are ye when men shall revile you and persecute you, and shall say all manner of evil against you falsely, for my sake. Rejoice and be exceeding glad: for great is your reward in heaven."

To be a member of a church is the "in" thing today. In many places, it is almost a must for the respected businessman or executive to be able to add church membership to his list of credentials. A politician, too, knows that he becomes more believable if he can add "member of so-and-so church" after his name.

But what of the churches of today? What is their function? Are they concerned for the lost? Many of them are no more than social clubs where members gather to see or be seen, their consciences soothed by mere attendance. But what of the church that Jesus built, the church that He commissioned to evangelize the world? Where are the committed disciples who "turned the world upside down" for their faith? Where are the martyrs, those willing to die for their convictions?

As I was listening to a news story on the radio, my ears pricked up when the news announcer reported that a certain man in a certain foreign country had been arrested and accused of being a Christian. That was all he said, and I never did hear any follow-up reports. I've thought about that news story since and wondered whether or not he was convicted. Was there enough evidence against him that beyond a shadow of a doubt he was convicted of being a Christian?

That news story made me stop and think about myself. If I were arrested and accused of being a Christian, would there be enough evidence to convict me in a court of law? Can others see the evidence of Jesus in my life? Does my life display the qualities of Christ? Or is my faith so shallow that a good defense attorney could get me off for lack of evidence? What a sobering thought!

God's Reaction to Shallow Faith

There was a time when the Father called His ministers together and bestowed upon them gifts according to their individual burdens and abilities. To one, He gave two; and to another, five sermons to preach. To another, He gave one sermon to preach. He told them, "I am entrusting each of you with My words of wisdom and comfort. Go and preach these messages so that My salvation story can reach the lost."

The Father went away, and the preachers were left to carry out His wishes. After a period of time, the Father returned and once again assembled together His ministers, checking on their progress.

To the one who had been given five sermons, He said, "I entrusted you with five messages. Give Me a report on what you did with what I gave you."

The preacher said, "Father, You gave me five sermons to preach. I went to my home church where I am pastor and preached these five messages to my people. Then, after preaching them, a burden for the lost compelled me to go to the evangelistic field, where I again preached these five messages. Therefore, Your five sermons were turned into ten, doubling what You gave me."

The Father said, "Well done, good and faithful preacher. Because you have been a wise steward over My gifts and have increased by twofold what I gave you, I will bless your ministry by filling your mind to overflowing with new ideas and thoughts for many sermons, thereby increasing your effectiveness to a lost and dying world."

Likewise, to the preacher who had been given two messages to preach, the Father said, "Give Me a report on what you did with the two sermons I entrusted to you."

"Father, I, too, preached the two messages You gave me to my home church. Then, one of the neighboring pastors heard about the impact of these two sermons on my city and invited me to come and preach them to his congregation. Therefore, the two sermons You gave me were turned into four, thereby increasing their effectiveness twofold."

The Father said, "Well done, good and faithful preacher. Because you have been faithful over a few things, I will bless your ministry by filling your mind with many more creative thoughts for new sermons, whereby you will be able to reach out and win many souls for My kingdom."

Then, to the preacher who had been entrusted with one message, the Father asked, "And what did you do with the one sermon I gave you?"

"Father, I wrote the sermon out just like You gave it to me, but because I was afraid of rejection if I preached it, I put it in a desk drawer and saved it until Your return, knowing that You are wise and merciful and would understand. See, Father, here's the sermon You gave me, neatly typed and still intact," said the preacher waving a sheaf of papers.

The Father said, "Oh, you unprofitable preacher! I entrusted you with My words of salvation, comfort, and inspiration, but because of your fear of rejection you buried them in a desk drawer. This message I gave you was so powerful that, had you preached it, your church building could not have contained the new people that would have flocked there. It had such a drawing effect that, had you preached it, your city would have been turned upside down for the gospel.

"Unfortunately, because your fear of rejection was greater than your trust in Me, I will empty your mind of any creative thoughts. I will take this one message from you and give it to the preacher who turned five sermons into ten and to the one who turned two sermons into four. Their ministries will flourish and receive acclaim and recognition, not necessarily because they are more talented, but simply because they are more willing."

God's How-to Book

Before a person can become a committed disciple, he must first become acquainted with God's written Word. In our modern and complex world there are many books written on various do-it-yourself projects. According to the authors, we can build our own house, doctor our own cat, repair our own car, and be our own lawyer. There are books on "How to Be Your Own Boss," "How to Make Your Own Clothes," "How to Win Friends," "How to Achieve Success," "How to Grow Rich," and many more "How-to" topics.

A book written long ago deals with "How to Be Saved." It is God's Word, the Bible. However, salvation is not a do-it-yourself project. We do not earn salvation by merit, but we receive it by grace through faith. It is God's way and not our way. When we activate our faith by obedience to God's plan, then God gives us the gift of salvation.

Some church groups reject the deity of Christ, but the Bible clearly states that the fullness of God dwells in Him. Other religious movements teach many gods, but God plainly says in the Bible, "Is there a God beside me? yea, there is no God; I know not any" (Isaiah 44:8). Others teach that good works are the vehicle by which to enter heaven, but God's Word states, "By grace are ye saved . . . not of works, lest any man should boast" (Ephesians 2:8-9).

Salvation is a free gift of God. No one can earn it; if he did, then he could boast that he did it himself. Cornelius was a devout man, a man who prayed, and a man of many good works, yet his devotion, prayers, and good deeds did not save him. God sent Peter to tell him how to be saved (Acts 11:13-15). Salvation is not a do-it-yourself program.

The Bible is complete—God's whole message to man.

The Bible is God's revealed will to humanity and the highest source of divine authority. No one has the privilege to create his own doctrine; rather, the Bible establishes what every person must believe and obey. "Do it yourself" must yield to the "do it God's way" of Holy Writ.

The Bible reveals Jesus Christ as God's redemptive plan. Symbols and ceremonies in the Old Testament become reality in the Cross and empty tomb. Types and shadows in the Old Testament become truth and substance in the New Testament. Jesus, the theme of the entire Bible, is a thread woven through all the Scriptures. To unravel that thread is to discover Jesus—the way, the truth, and the life. To become acquainted with Him is to know God, for He is "God with us." Jesus said, "Search the scriptures; for in them ye think ye have eternal life: and they are they which testify of me" (John 5:39).

The people who believe the message of Jesus in the Bible and experience the salvation He provides through the Cross become different. "All things are become new" (II Corinthians 5:17). Rich or poor, young or old, from any country in the world, sinners are converted to become sons and daughters of God. Even their speech habits change, for their thoughts and inner feelings take on the presence of God's holiness. Their entire outlook on living radiates with heavenly grace and splendor.

Learn to Communicate

A committed disciple is one who learns to communicate with the Lord. To communicate implies the ability to relate to another our innermost feelings, learning to impart our innermost self to Him and learning to recognize His voice as he imparts His innermost self to us.

Real communication with our Lord requires listening. We tend to do all the talking instead of quietly listening as God attempts to talk to us.

To open the doors of communication with God, we must bring our thoughts together and be still before the Lord. We need a quiet time alone with God, a definite time period every day for quiet reading of God's Word, meditation upon that Word, talking to the Lord, and letting Him talk to us. A quiet place is also beneficial. Solitude is not necessarily a place but a state of heart and mind. As we learn to communicate with God, we will discover that prayer does not need a geographical spot but rather a willing state of mind and heart.

Through His Word

The more time we spend with the Lord, the more we learn to recognize His voice. We find that He speaks to us in many ways. He speaks through thoughts, impressions, and even silence. As we spend time before Him in prayer listening, we learn to recognize the gentle nudgings of His Spirit when He speaks through His Word, through others, through circumstances, and through His Spirit.

In order to hear what God is saying when he speaks through His Word, an involved listener is always probing, searching, and comparing. He thinks constantly, How can I apply this to my life? What principle is God showing me?

Through the principles of the Bible, even when God's Word is silent on a particular issue, the perceptive listener will hear God speak. Applying these principles to every issue of life, we hear God's voice speaking even through His silence.

Through Others

When God chooses to speak to us through godly people, what we hear could be just a simple word in passing but could alter the course of our lives. If God chooses to speak in this way, a stirring witness inside our heart will confirm that God is truly speaking to us.

Some years ago God spoke directly to me through my pastor. My pastor was not speaking directly to me, however, but rather to a new lady praying at the altar. I was close enough to hear him tell her, "You have no control over tomorrow; quit living your life ten years in the future. Live one day at a time." I was shocked as I listened to his words—shocked because for weeks I had been painstakingly committing to paper what I intended for my life for the next ten years. I had listed each of the ten years separately and alongside them had listed my plans for that year. No one knew this but me . . . and God. Knowing in my heart that God had truly spoken to me, I went home and tore up my list. Not long afterward, my future collapsed and those ten-year plans instantly dissolved when I became a widow. Learning to recognize God's voice through someone else helps to prepare us for what is to come.

Through Circumstances

When God speaks to us through circumstances, such circumstances take on many forms. Sometimes it is through financial collapse; sometimes it is an illness; sometimes a disappointment; sometimes a tragedy. God uses all circumstances in life to speak to us. Whether or not we hear God's voice speaking through circumstances will be affected not only by our relationship with Him but also by another factor—our understanding of who He is. How do we view God? Faithful, just, kind? Or demanding, intolerant, distant? We must understand the character of the God we serve before we can really hear Him speak through the circumstances of our lives.

Through His Spirit

When God speaks to us by His Spirit, He will often bring to mind particular areas of our lives that need changing. Because He loves us, He wants to cleanse us. That is when we either run away or develop our relationship with Him. No doubt, ongoing personal cleansing was one of the chief attributes that made David a man after God's own heart. Rather than run from God's searching light, David humbled himself and became broken before the Lord.

When we allow ourselves to be thus disciplined and broken by the Spirit of God, He communicates His will to us. Only from a life spent "dwelling in the secret place of the most High" (Psalm 91:1) can we become a committed disciple.

When "Men Revile You"

To revile means to verbally abuse. Jesus said we are "blessed" when we're talked about, made fun of, and laughed at for His sake.

The life we live before people determines whether we have shallow faith (for which if we are arrested and accused of being a Christian there will not be enough evidence to convict us) or are committed disciples (for which we will surely be ridiculed, laughed at, and talked about). If we are persecuted for His sake, we are to count it all joy! Jesus said, "Rejoice." We are "blessed"! Great is our reward in heaven!

"Blessed are ye, when men shall revile you, and persecute you, and shall say all manner of evil against you falsely, for my sake. Rejoice, and be exceeding glad: for great is your reward in heaven."

Summary

True or False

1. Some people want to be a member of a church only as a status symbol.
2. A martyr is a person whose beliefs are not very strong.
3. The church that was commissioned to evangelize the world consisted of committed disciples who turned their world upside down.
4. It's okay to bury God's gifts if we have a good reason.
5. Salvation is earned by merit.
6. Those who believe and obey the Bible are changed to radiate God's grace.
7. The more we have communication with our Lord the more we will become confused.
8. When the Bible is silent on a particular issue, we are then free to indulge in or refrain from the issue, whichever we choose.
9. God speaks to us through His Word.
10. We will be "reviled" (talked about, laughed at, and ridiculed) if we follow Jesus closely.

Answers

1. True, 2. False, 3. True, 4. False, 5. False, 6. True, 7. False, 8. False, 9. True, 10. True,

11

Jesus' Beautiful Attitudes: Accomplishing the Goal

The magician and conjurer of old was a master of illusion and deception. By his movements, he distracted attention from the real. The insignificant movement of one hand focused attention on the false, while the other hand calmly concealed the real.

Likewise, the master conjurer of this world has created an illusion. What we see is not really what is. The things we think are, are not, and what we think are not, really are.

By his movements, the master conjurer has focused the attention of God's people on the world's standards and has tried to conceal the real—Jesus' standards. It's all an illusion, a deception, a created image.

The conjurer focuses attention on the insignificant to hide the significant; on the negative to hide the positive; on weakness to hide strength. By stripping away these illusions or created images, we see the real. What seems to be impossible is possible; what seems to be weakness is strength; what seems to be doubt is faith; what seems to be defeat is victory.

Steps to Accomplished Goals

It is interesting that Jesus told us what "beautiful attitudes" to exemplify and that in so doing we would be blessed (happy), but He didn't tell us how to achieve them. The method of achieving them is perhaps the same method used in achieving any goal. The steps are:

1. Desire
2. Sacrifice
3. Time
4. Responsibility
5. Commitment
6. Perseverance

Desire

The first step in accomplishing any goal is desire and the motivation to carry it through to completion. Without desire, Jesus' attitudes will lie dormant in our lives. They do not happen accidentally. They must be cultivated and developed through desire and motivation.

Motivation is an idea, need, or emotion that prompts an action. Action is the end result of motivation and desire. Real motivation comes from within and is a part of our innermost thoughts.

Motivation comes about through daily repetition: feeding the brain with habits, thought patterns, and desires. Our thoughts become actions, actions become habits, and habits grow into character.

Why is it easy for an honest person to be honest? Because he has daily practiced being honest.

Why is it easy for some people to tell the truth? Because they habitually do it.

Why is it easy for the man who gets up at six o'clock every morning to continue to get up at that hour? Because of repetition. It has become a habit.

These things may be hard at first, but when the habit has been formed then it is hard to do otherwise. A continuously repeated activity becomes so ingrained in our nature that it is almost involuntary. We develop motivation by doing what ought to be done when it ought to be done, whether we like it or not.

Sacrifice

Sacrifice is the next step in accomplishing a goal—the sacrifice of time, energy, self, and money. Sacrifice implies not being deterred from the goal. Sacrifice suggests someone who is consistent and not wishy-washy.

A medical student intent on graduation is prepared to sacrifice time, energy, and money to realize his goal. Nothing required of him is too much of a sacrifice (long hours of study, tedious and exacting lab work, never-ending expenses), because he can see the end from the beginning.

A person can accomplish his goal if he works for it, plans for it, and sacrifices for it. If a person will not sacrifice, we can say the desire was not strong enough. If desire is strong and motivation is developed, sacrifice will follow.

Time

Nothing worthwhile is accomplished overnight. We must give ourselves time.

One day we look in the mirror and don't like what we see. Pudginess has replaced slimness. What do we do? Most of us resolve to go on a diet to shed the unwanted pounds. With that goal in mind we set about to accomplish it. However, when we do not shed the extra pounds within two days we throw up our hands, relinquish our goal, and become resigned to living with our pudgy selves. But unwanted pounds are not gained in two days; neither will they be lost in two days. The world did not erect its false walls in our lives overnight; neither will they be torn down overnight. It takes time.

To accomplish any goal, we must have a realistic view of the time required.

Responsibility

Chaos will erupt without responsible living: responsibility in lifestyle, responsibility toward others, responsibility toward God. Irresponsibility is the breeding ground of negative forces. God's positive forces are rooted in responsible living.

Responsibility means accountability. We are held accountable for our actions. Through accountability we learn to make right decisions, stand on our own two feet, and live responsibly.

Responsibility also means discipline. Self-discipline simply reinforces established rules; it reinforces standards of conduct established by God. Through self-discipline we learn to make right decisions and to reinforce God's code of conduct, thereby stripping away the world's standards and living by God's standards.

Commitment

Commitment to a goal, to a purpose, to an idea, to

God, is necessary in reaching any goal. Commitment implies being consistent. Being consistent means unwavering, unchanging, undeterred.

Commitment suggests stability, which is the quality of being steadfast of purpose. Commitment is determination. Commitment is loyalty. Commitment is not being swayed by circumstances, personal feelings, or popular opinion.

Commitment does not accept or believe destructive criticism, gossip, or rumors, but it exhibits trust and confidence.

Commitment takes a definite determination and a strong will-power; however, the blessings and rewards make it well worth the effort.

Perseverance

All other steps to accomplishing a goal would fall by the wayside if it were not for this final step—perseverance. Perseverance is the ability to endure when things get tough. Perseverance does not necessarily mean endurance without progress. Perseverance means the ability to progress toward the stated goal even through adversity. When adversity comes (and it will), as we persevere we are not merely marking time but are doing something constructive to advance toward our objective.

Perseverance means the ability to buck a strong head wind and not be blown away by it; it means the ability to advance through the head wind. Advancing through a head wind is, of necessity, slow but through perseverance there is an advance and not a retreat. The attribute that turns an ordinary individual into a champion is perseverance, a fighting spirit that keeps on going through adversity. He just won't quit!

I heard the story of a young man who wanted to be the best rifle shot in the world and was in training for the 1948 World Olympics. In 1946, two years from the Olympics, he was in a tragic accident that cut off his right arm. Two years later at the World Olympics when the gold medal was presented for marksmanship, a one-armed man walked to the platform and received the gold medal. In two years he trained his opposite eye, he trained the arm that was of no use, and he went to the winners' circle. He took weakness and turned it into strength. He took failure and turned it into success. He took defeat and turned it into victory.

Conclusion

Experts declare that only ten percent of the people in America have an ultimate aim, a genuine motive for living. This is the great tragedy of American life. The person who has no objective is going nowhere. He is just drifting, and consequently, he never arrives.

Someone without an ultimate aim has a negative attitude, but someone with a definite purpose has a conquering spirit. He sets the pace; he leads the way; he has a vision. He knows which way he is traveling, and he knows why. He can see the end from the beginning because he can picture it in his imagination.

Why is it that one person has magnetism and another does not? Why is it that one person has a distinct personality and another does not? Why is it that one person radiates courage, optimism, enthusiasm, ambition, and leadership and another does not? It is because one has anchored his life with a definite aim, an ultimate purpose, and the other has not. That aim creates within him life's great positive forces.

The person who has a definite aim in life grasps every opportunity that will help him achieve his end. The person who drifts has no aim and therefore sees no opportunities.

To acquire the desirable things of life, a person must first decide what he wants. When he once chooses his purpose and fortifies it by a burning, conquering determination, he will begin to study ways and means for reaching his goal.

When a person once decides upon an objective, he expects to make sacrifices. He meets difficulties with eagerness. He is willing to endure almost any hardship in order to accomplish his purpose. People do not understand him because they cannot see his dominating, impelling motive.

The aim and goal of every child of God should create an inner, compelling motivating force to tear down the false walls of created images that the world has erected, strip away the facade to expose the inner person Jesus intended us to be, and then exemplify those "beautiful attitudes" to others.

In the process, we must expect to see wounds. Nothing worthwhile is accomplished unless there is a battle, and in every battle there are wounds: wounded spirits, wounded emotions, wounded personalities, wounded thoughts.

We treasure our cleverness, thinking we are quite important; we treasure our own emotions and feelings; we esteem ourselves superior to others; we fret over trifles; we murmur at small losses. In other words, we focus on ourselves. But then, attempting to emulate Jesus' teachings, we decide to offer ourselves to the Lord to be at His service. When we offer ourselves to the Lord, we cannot afford to be lenient or to spare ourselves. We must allow the Lord to work in our lives, to utterly strip away the world's false wall. In so doing, there will be wounds. It will hurt!

When we offer ourselves to God, He takes the hammer and the chisel rips out the nails of self-love, pride, discontent, haughtiness. He lays our life alongside the perfect pattern and begins to cut away the superfluous. Oh, how it hurts! He takes the needle and thread of the Spirit and stitches for us His wedding garment. In making the wedding garment, we must expect to see wounds, but the end result will be glorious.

"And I heard as it were the voice of a great multitude, and as the voice of many waters, and as the voice of mighty thunderings, saying, Alleluia: for the Lord God omnipotent reigneth. Let us be glad and rejoice, and give honour to him: for the marriage of the Lamb is come, and his wife hath made herself ready. And to her was granted that she should be arrayed in fine linen, clean and white: for the fine linen is the righteousness of saints" (Revelation 19:6-8).